Chicago Cubs 2019

A Baseball Companion

Edited by Patrick Dubuque, Aaron Gleeman and Bret Sayre

Baseball Prospectus

Craig Brown and Dave Pease, Consultant Editors
Rob McQuown and Harry Pavlidis, Statistics Editors

Copyright © 2019 by DIY Baseball, LLC.
All rights reserved

This book or any part thereof may not be reproduced or transmitted in any form or by any means, electronic or mechanical, including photocopying, recording, or by any information storage and retrieval system, without permission in writing from the publisher.

Limit of Liability/Disclaimer of Warranty: While the publisher and the author have used their best efforts in preparing this book, they make no representations or warranties with respect to the accuracy or completeness of the contents of this book and specifically disclaim any implied warranties of merchantability or fitness for a particular purpose. No warranty may be created or extended by sales representatives or written sales materials. The advice and strategies contained herein may not be suitable for your situation. You should consult with a professional where appropriate. Neither the publisher nor the author shall be liable for any loss of profit or any other commercial damages, including but not limited to special, incidental, consequential, or other damages.

Library of Congress Cataloging-in-Publication Data:
paperback
ISBN-13: 978-1-949332-34-6

Project Credits
Cover Design: Kathleen Dyson
Interior Design and Production: Jeff Pease, Dave Pease
Layout: Jeff Pease, Dave Pease

Baseball icon courtesy of Uberux, from https://www.shareicon.net/author/uberux

Ballpark diagram courtesy of Lou Spirito/THIRTY81 Project, https://thirty81project.com/

Manufactured in the United States of America
10 9 8 7 6 5 4 3 2 1

Table of Contents

Foreword v
    Rob Mains

Statistical Introduction vii

Part 1: Team Analysis

Table for Three: Previewing the 2019 Chicago Cubs 3
    Josh Cole, Sam Fels and Zack Moser

Performance Graphs 9

2018 Team Performance 10

2019 Team Projections 11

Team Personnel 12

Wrigley Field Stats 13

Cubs Team Analysis 15

Part 2: Player Analysis

Cubs Player Analysis 22

Cubs Prospects 103

Part 3: Featured Articles

The Hole in The Shift is Fixing Itself 115
    Russell Carleton

The State of the Quality Start 119
    Rob Mains

Heads-Up Hacking—The First Pitch 125
    Matthew Trueblood

A Hymn for the Index Stat 131
    Patrick Dubuque

Index of Names 135

Foreword

Rob Mains

Welcome to this companion of the 2019 Chicago Cubs. We at Baseball Prospectus are excited to provide this analysis of the Cubs.

Our website, Baseball Prospectus, is a leader in delivering high-quality commentary and data to baseball fans everywhere. To some, those words—commentary and data—appear mutually exclusive. There are people out there who believe that traditional analysis and advanced analytics must run on different paths. But the simplistic narrative of stats vs. traditionalists just isn't true. Every team's analytics department interacts with scouting, development, and major league operations with a common goal: Delivering a championship. New technologies, like radar tracking of pitch speeds and movement, enable talent evaluators to focus on qualitative aspects of pitching like mechanics and pitch sequencing. In-game strategies like infield shifts, based on batters' hit tendencies, help turn balls in play into outs. Hitters use information to adjust their swings to maximize run production.

All these numbers can seem, at best, intimidating, and at worst, counterproductive to the casual fan. Even as technology and analysis have embedded themselves deeply into the way teams run, it can often feel like statistics create a displacement between the viewer and the sport, breaking them out of the action. And yet every fan incorporates the numbers to some degree; stats like batting average and earned run average, so fundamental to how we talk about performance, are actually complicated formulas. They don't bother people because those formulas have become second nature, as easy to translate as the action on the field.

Along the way, new statistics have entered baseball's lexicon. You'll see some of them, like on-base percentage (which measures a batter's ability to get on base via walk, hit batter, or hit), OPS (on-base plus slugging), and average exit velocity (the speed of balls off a hitter's bat) on broadcasts. Others, like DRC+, might well be new to you. Some of them have been well-defined to the public, others haven't. That lack of context has created ambiguity. Fans know that a ball hit 100 mph is scorched, but does that mean extra bases? (Not if it's hit on the ground or high in the air it doesn't.)

For those who are amenable to them, the new statistics can increase the enjoyment and understanding of the game. They can help fans identify when a pitcher is tiring, when a stolen base or a bunt attempt makes sense (and, more often, when it doesn't), or how a team's lineup might be constructed. Websites like Baseball Prospectus add to that understanding by weaving metrics into the narrative of the game. That's the goal of this publication: to take some of the newer, more complicated statistics and make them as intuitive as the ones on the back of old baseball cards.

But you don't need to love analytics to love baseball. The fans at BP who worked together to write this guide are captivated first and foremost by the game itself. We're drawn to Aaron Judge's power, Francisco Lindor's glove, Billy Hamilton's speed and Patrick Corbin's slider and don't need numbers to tell us why they're so mesmerizing. The underlying statistics provide depth to the game that we all love.

We hope you'll find that this guide helps you better understand the Cubs. Our analysts have studied the team's major league personnel and its minor league affiliates to identify their strengths and weaknesses, both the obvious ones and those that only a careful dissection of players' performances—yes, including the data—can reveal. You don't need us to tell you who was good and who wasn't in 2018, but our models and writers can help you project how each player is going to perform this year and beyond, and appreciate the greatness of each new game as it unfolds. As in the sport itself, the human and analytic components combine to generate a deeper overall understanding.

Think back to the first time you saw a baseball game on a high-definition TV. You'd grown familiar with how the game looked and felt on a picture tube. But new TV allowed you to see details that you'd never seen before. That's how advanced statistics work. The game itself is why you're here and why you're buying this. (And, for that matter, why we wrote it.) The statistical measures provide the sharper focus, the detail, the depth of knowledge that you didn't have before, generating an overall superior picture. Enjoy the view.

—Rob Mains is an author of Baseball Prospectus.

Statistical Introduction

Sports are, fundamentally, a blend of athletic endeavor and storytelling. Baseball, like any other sport, tells its stories in so many ways: in the arc of a game from the stands or a season from the box scores, in photos, or even in numbers. At Baseball Prospectus, we understand that statistics don't replace observation or any of baseball's stories, but complement everything else that makes the game so much fun.

What stats help us with is with patterns and precision, variance and value. This book can help you learn things you may not see from watching a game or hundred, whether it's the path of a career over time or the breadth of the entire MLB. We'd also never ask you to choose between our numbers and the experience of viewing a game from the cheap seats or the comfort of your home; our publication combines running the numbers with observations and wisdom from some of the brightest minds we can find. But if you *do* want to learn more about the numbers beyond what's on the backs of player jerseys, let us help explain.

Offense

At the end of this past year, we've revised our methodology for determining batting value. Long-time readers of Baseball Prospectus will notice that we've retired True Average in favor of a new metric: Deserved Runs Created Plus (DRC+). Developed by Jonathan Judge and our stats team, this statistic measures everything a player does at the plate–reaching base, hitting for power, making outs, and moving runners over–and puts it on a scale where 100 equals league-average performance. A DRC+ of 150 is terrific, a DRC+ of 100 is average, and a DRC+ of 75 means you better be an excellent defender.

DRC+ also does a better job than any of our previous metrics in taking contextual factors into account. The model adjusts for how the park affects performance, but also for things like the talent of the opposing pitcher, value of different types of batted-ball events, league, temperature, and other factors. It's able to describe a player's expected offensive contribution than any other statistic we've found over the years, and also does a better job of predicting future performance as well.

The other aspect of run-scoring is baserunning, which we quantify using Baserunning Runs. BRR not only records the value of stolen bases (or getting caught in the act), but also accounts for a runner's ability to go first to third on a single or advance on a fly ball.

Defense

Where offensive value is *relatively* easy to identify and understand, defensive value is ... not. Over the past dozen years, the sabermetric community has focused mostly on stats based on zone data: a real-live human person records the type of batted ball and estimated landing location, and models are created that give expected outs. From there, you can compare fielders' actual outs to those expected ones. Simple, right?

Unfortunately, zone data has two major issues. First, zone data is recorded by commercial data providers who keep the raw data private unless you pay for it. (All the statistics we build in this book and on our website use public data as inputs.) That hurts our ability to test assumptions or duplicate results. Second, over the years it has become apparent that there's quite a bit of "noise" in zone-based fielding analysis. Sometimes the conclusions drawn from zone data don't hold up to scrutiny, and sometimes the different data provided by different providers don't look anything alike, giving wildly different results. Sometimes the hard-working professional stringers or scorers might unknowingly inflict unconscious bias into the mix: for example good fielders will often be credited with more expected outs despite the data, and ballparks with high press boxes tend to score more line drives than ones with a lower press box.

Enter our Fielding Runs Above Average (FRAA). For most positions, FRAA is built from play-by-play data, which allows us to avoid the subjectivity found in many other fielding metrics. The idea is this: count how many fielding plays are made by a given player and compare that to expected plays for an average fielder at their position (based on pitcher ground-ball tendencies and batter handedness). Then we adjust for park and base-out situations.

When it comes to catchers, our methodology is a little different thanks to the laundry list of responsibilities they're tasked with beyond just, well, catching and throwing the ball. By now you've probably heard about "framing" or the art of making umpires more likely to call balls outside the strike zone for strikes. To put this into one tidy number, we incorporate pitch tracking data (for the years it exists) and adjust for important factors like pitcher, umpire, batter, and home-field advantage using a mixed-model approach. This grants us a number for how many strikes the catcher is personally adding to (or subtracting from) his pitchers' performance ... which we then convert to runs added or lost using linear weights.

Framing is one of the biggest parts of determining catcher value, but we also take into account blocking balls from going past, whether a scorer deems it a passed ball or a wild pitch. We use a similar approach–one that really benefits from the pitch tracking data that tells us what ends up in the dirt and what doesn't. We also include a catcher's ability to prevent stolen bases and how well they field balls in play, and *finally* we come up with our FRAA for catchers.

Pitching

Both pitching and fielding make up the half of baseball that isn't run scoring: run prevention. Separating pitching from fielding is a tough task, and most recent pitching analysis has branched off from Voros McCracken's famous (and controversial) statement, "There is little if any difference among major-league pitchers in their ability to prevent hits on balls hit in the field of play." The research of the analytic community has validated this to some extent, and there are a host of "defense-independent" pitching measures that have been developed to try and extricate the effect of the defense behind a hurler from the pitcher's work.

Our solution to this quandry is Deserved Run Average (DRA), our core pitching metric. DRA looks like earned run average (ERA), the tried-and-true pitching stat you've seen on every baseball broadcast or box score from the past century, but it's very different. To start, DRA takes an event-by-event look at what the pitchers does, and adjusts the value of that event based on different environmental factors like park, batter, catcher, umpire, base-out situation, run differential, inning, defense, home field advantage, pitcher role, and temperature. That mixed model gives us a pitcher's expected contribution, similar to what we do for our DRC+ model for hitters and FRAA model for catchers. (Oh, and we also consider the pitcher's effect on basestealing and on balls getting past the catcher.)

It's important to note that DRA is set to the scale of runs allowed per nine innings (RA9) instead of ERA, which makes DRA's scale slightly higher than ERA's. The reason for this is because ERA tends to overrate three types of pitchers:

1. Pitchers who play in parks where scorers hand out more errors. Official scorers differ significantly in the frequency at which they assign errors to fielders.
2. Ground-ball pitchers, because a substantial proportion of errors occur on grounders.
3. Pitchers who aren't very good. Better pitchers often allow fewer unearned runs than bad pitchers, because good pitchers tend to find ways to get out of jams.

Since the last time you picked up an edition of this book, we've also made a few minor changes to DRA to make it better. Recent research into "tunneling"–the act of throwing consecutive pitches that appear similar from a batter's point of view until after the swing decision point–data has given us a new contextual factor to account for in DRA: plate distance. This refers to the distance between successive pitches as they approach the plate, and while it has a smaller effect than factors like velocity or whiff rate, it still can help explain pitcher strikeout rate in our model.

New Pitching Metrics for 2019

We're including a few "new" pitching metrics for 2019's suite of Baseball Prospectus publications, but you may be familiar with them if you've spent time scouring the internet for stats.

Fastball Percentage

Our fastball percentage (FB%) statistic measures how frequently a pitcher throws a pitch classified as a "fastball," measured as a percentage of overall pitches thrown. We qualify three types of fastballs:

1. The traditional four-seam fastball;
2. The two-seam fastball or sinker;
3. "Hard cutters," which are pitches that have the movement profile of a cut fastball and are used as the pitcher's primary offering or in place of a more traditional fastball.

For example, a pitcher with a FB% of 67 throws any combination of these three pitches about two-thirds of the time.

Whiff Rate

Everybody loves a swing and a miss, and whiff rate (WHF) measures how frequently pitchers induce a swinging strike. To calculate WHF, we add up all the pitches thrown that ended with a swinging strike, then divide that number by a pitcher's total pitches thrown. Most often, high whiff rates correlate with high strikeout rates (and overall effective pitcher performance).

Called Strike Probability

Called Strike Probability (CSP) is a number that represents the likelihood that all of a pitcher's pitches will be called a strike while controlling for location, pitcher and batter handedness, umpire and count. Here's how it works: on each pitch, our model determines how many times (out of 100) that a similar pitch was called for a strike given those factors mentioned above, and when normalized for each batter's strike zone. Then we average the CSP for all pitches thrown by a pitcher in a season, and that gives us the yearly CSP percentage you see in the stats boxes.

As you might imagine, pitchers with a higher CSP are more likely to work in the zone, where pitchers with a lower CSP are likely locating their pitches outside the normal strike zone, for better or for worse.

Projections

Many of you aren't turning to this book just for a look at what a player has done, but for a look at what a player is going to do: the PECOTA projections. PECOTA, initially developed by Nate Silver (who has moved on to greater fame as a political analyst), consists of three parts:

1. Major-league equivalencies, which use minor-league statistics to project how a player will perform in the major leagues;
2. Baseline forecasts, which use weighted averages and regression to the mean to estimate a player's current true talent level; and
3. Aging curves, which uses the career paths of comparable players to estimate how a player's statistics are likely to change over time.

With all those important things covered, let's take a look at what's in the book this year.

Team Prospectus

You bought this book to learn more about your favorite (or maybe least-favorite, who are we to judge?) team, so let's talk about them. After a thoughtful preview of the 2019 season, you'll be presented with our Team Prospectus. This outlines many of the key statistics for each team's 2018 season, as well as a very inviting stadium diagram.

First you'll find the Performance Graphs page. The first is the 2018 Hit List Ranking. This shows our Hit List Rank for the team on each day of the 2018 season and is intended to give you a picture of the ups and downs of the team's season, including their highest and lowest ranks of the year. Hit List Rank measures overall team performance and drives the Hit List Power Rankings at the baseballprospectus.com website.

The second graph is Committed Payroll and helps you see how the team's payroll has compared to the MLB and divisional average payrolls over time. Payroll figures are currents as of January 1, 2019; with so many free agents still unsigned as of this writing, the final 2018 figure will likely be significantly different for many teams. (In the meantime, you can always find the most current data at Baseball Prospectus' Cot's Baseball Contracts page.)

The third graph is Farm System Ranking and displays how the Baseball Prospectus prospect team has ranked the organization's farm system since 2007. It also indicates the highest and lowest ranks that the farm system achieved over that time.

We start the Team Performance page with the squad's unadjusted and third-order 2018 win-loss records, presented in divisional context. We then list the three highest performing hitters and pitchers by WARP for 2018. Beneath that are a host of other team statistics. **Pythag** presents an adjusted 2018 winning percentage, calculated by taking runs scored per game (**RS/G**) and runs allowed per game (**RA/G**) for the team, and running them through a version of Bill James' Pythagorean formula that was refined and improved by David Smyth and Brandon Heipp. (The formula is called "Pythagenpat," which is equally fun to type and to say.)

Next up is **DRC+**, described earlier, to indicate the overall hitting ability of the team either above or below league-average. Run prevention on the pitching side is covered by **DRA** (also mentioned earlier) and another metric: Fielding Independent Pitching (**FIP**), which calculates another ERA-like statistic based on strikeouts, walks, and home runs recorded. Defensive Efficiency Rating (**DER**) tells us the percentage of balls in play turned into outs for the team, and is a quick fielding shorthand that rounds out run prevention.

After that, we have several measures related to roster composition, as opposed to on-field performance. **B-Age** and **P-Age** tell us the average age of a team's batters and pitchers, respectively. **Salary** is the combined team payroll for all on-field players, and Doug Pappas' Marginal Dollars per Marginal Win (**M$/MW**) tells us how much money a team spent to earn production above replacement level.

Ending this batch of statistics is the number of disabled list days a team had over the season (**DL Days**) and the amount of salary paid to players on the disabled list (**$ on DL**); this final number is expressed as a percentage of total payroll.

Next to each of these stats, we've listed each team's MLB rank in that category from 1st to 30th. In this, 1st always indicates a positive outcome and 30th a negative outcome, except in the case of salary–1st is highest.

The Team Projections page is intended to convey the team's operational capacity entering the 2019 season. We start with the team's PECOTA projected record for 2019, again in divisional context. The **+/-** column indicates how many more or less wins the team is projected to get than they got in 2018. We then list the three highest projected hitters and pitchers by WARP for 2018. A brief farm system summary follows, with the team's top prospect and number of BP Top 101 Prospects. Finally, we list the key new players and departed players, along with their 2019 projected WARP.

Alex Bregman 3B

Born: 03/30/94 Age: 25 Bats: R Throws: R
Height: 6'0" Weight: 180 Origin: Round 1, 2015 Draft (#2 overall)

YEAR	TEAM	LVL	AGE	PA	R	2B	3B	HR	RBI	BB	K	SB	CS	AVG/OBP/SLG
2016	CCH	AA	22	285	54	16	2	14	46	42	26	5	3	.297/.415/.559
2016	FRE	AAA	22	83	17	6	0	6	15	5	12	2	1	.333/.373/.641
2016	HOU	MLB	22	217	31	13	3	8	34	15	52	2	0	.264/.313/.478
2017	HOU	MLB	23	626	88	39	5	19	71	55	97	17	5	.284/.352/.475
2018	HOU	MLB	24	705	105	51	1	31	103	96	85	10	4	.286/.394/.532
2019	HOU	MLB	25	675	96	38	3	23	78	73	107	12	4	.272/.359/.463

Breakout: 6% Improve: 52% Collapse: 5% Attrition: 2% MLB: 100%
Comparables: Anthony Rendon, David Wright, Pablo Sandoval

YEAR	TEAM	LVL	AGE	PA	DRC+	VORP	BABIP	BRR	FRAA	WARP
2016	CCH	AA	22	285	172	38.9	.286	1.6	SS(51): -3.4, 3B(11): 1.4	2.7
2016	FRE	AAA	22	83	161	10.0	.333	-1.2	SS(14): 2.1, LF(3): -0.1	0.8
2016	HOU	MLB	22	217	107	9.6	.317	0.5	3B(40): 0.9, SS(6): -0.1	1.1
2017	HOU	MLB	23	626	114	34.7	.311	-1.5	3B(132): 8.7, SS(30): -2.9	3.9
2018	HOU	MLB	24	705	150	72.6	.289	-1.6	3B(136): 5.4, SS(28): -0.4	7.4
2019	HOU	MLB	25	675	125	37.3	.295	0.0	3B 7, SS 0	4.6

After the projections page, we share a few items about the team's home ballpark. There's the aforementioned diagram of the park's dimensions (including distances to the outfield wall), a few important biographical facts about the stadium, a graphic showing the height of the wall from the left-field pole to the right-field pole, and a table showing three-year park factors for the stadium. The park factors are displayed as indexes where 100 is average, 110 means that the park inflates the statistic in question by 10 percent, and 90 means that the park deflates the statistic in question by 10 percent.

Following the ballpark page, we have a **Personnel** section that lists many of the important decision-makers and upper-level field and operations staff members for the franchise, as well as any former Baseball Prospectus staff members who are currently part of the organization.

Position Players

After all that information and a thoughtful bylined essay covering each team, we present our player comments. Each player is listed with the major-league team who employed him as of early January 2019. If a player changed teams after that point via free agency, trade, or any other method, you'll be able to find them in the book for their previous squad.

First, we cover biographical information (age is as of June 30, 2019) before moving onto the stats themselves. Our statistic columns include standard identifying information like **YEAR**, **TEAM**, **LVL** (level of affiliated play) and **AGE** before getting into the numbers. Next, we provide raw, unstranslated numbers like you might find on the back of your dad's baseball cards: **PA** (plate appearances), **R** (runs), **2B** (doubles), **3B** (triples), **HR** (home runs), **RBI** (runs batted in), **BB** (walks), **K** (strikeouts), **SB** (stolen bases) and **CS** (caught stealing). Then we have unadjusted "slash" statistics: **AVG** (batting average), **OBP** (on-base percentage) and **SLG** (slugging percentage).

Just below the stats box is **PECOTA** data, which is discussed further in a following section. After that, it's on to a pithy and always-informative comment written by a member of the Baseball Prospectus staff, before we cover more stats.

The second text box repeats YEAR, TEAM, LVL, AGE, and PA, then moves on to **DRC+** (Deserved Runs Created Plus), which we described earlier as total offensive expected contribution compared to the league average. Next, one of our oldest active metrics, **VORP** (Value Over Replacement Player), considers offensive production, position and plate appearances. In essence, it is the number of runs contributed beyond what a replacement-level player at the same position would contribute if given the same percentage of team plate appearances. VORP does not consider the quality of a player's defense.

BABIP (batting average on balls in play) tells us how often a ball in play fell for a hit, and can help us identify whether a batter may have been lucky or not ... but note that high BABIPs also tend to follow the great hitters of our time, as well as speedy singles hitters who put the ball on the ground.

The next item is **BRR** (Baserunning Runs), which covers all of a player's baserunning accomplishments which includes (but isn't limited to) swiped bags and failed attempts. Next is **FRAA** (Fielding Runs Above Average), which also includes the number of games previously played at each position noted in parentheses. Multi-position players have only their two most frequent positions listed here, but their total FRAA number reflects all positions played.

Our last column here is **WARP** (Wins Above Replacement Player). WARP estimates the total value of a player, which means for hitters it takes into account hitting runs above average (calculated using the DRC+ model), BRR and FRAA. Then, it makes an adjustment for positions played and gives the player a credit for plate appearances based upon the difference between "replacement level"¬–which is derived from the quality of players added to a team's roster after the start of the season¬–and the league average.

Catchers

Catchers are a special breed, and thus they have earned their own separate box which displays some of the defensive metrics that we've built just for them. As an example, let's check out J.T. Realmuto.

YEAR	TEAM	P. COUNT	FRM RUNS	BLK RUNS	THRW RUNS	TOT RUNS
2016	MIA	18935	-8.5	1.8	2.1	-5.6
2017	MIA	18959	5.3	1.7	1.0	9.1
2018	MIA	16399	-0.4	0.9	0.1	0.4
2019	PHI	18448	-1.4	1.5	0.7	0.8

The **YEAR** and **TEAM** columns match what you'd find in the other stat box. **P. COUNT** indicates the number of pitches thrown while the catcher was behind the plate, including swinging strikes, fouls, and balls in play. **FRM RUNS** is the total run value the catcher provided (or cost) his team by influencing the umpire to call strikes where other catchers did not. **BLK RUNS** expresses the total run value above or below average for the catcher's ability to prevent wild pitches and passed balls. **THRW RUNS** is calculated using a similar model as the previous two statistics, and it measures a catcher's ability to throw out basestealers but also to dissuade them from testing his arm in the first place. It takes into account factors like the pitcher (including his delivery and pickoff move) and baserunner (who could be as fast as Billy Hamilton or as slow as Yonder Alonso). **TOT RUNS** is the sum of all of the previous three statistics.

Pitchers

Let's give our pitchers a turn, using 2018 NL Cy Young winner Jacob deGrom as our example. Take a look at his first stat block: the first line and the **YEAR**, **TEAM**, **LVL** and **AGE** columns are the same as in the position player example earlier.

Here too, we have a series of columns that display raw, unadjusted statistics compiled by the pitcher over the course of a season: **W** (wins), **L** (losses), **SV** (saves), **G** (games pitched), **GS** (games started), **IP** (innings pitched), **H** (hits allowed) and **HR** (home runs allowed). Next we have two statistics that are rates: **BB/9** (walks per nine innings) and **K/9** (strikeouts per nine innings), before returning to the unadjusted **K** (strikeouts).

Next up is **GB%** (ground ball percentage), which is the percentage of all batted balls that were hit in the ground, including both outs and hits. Remember, this is based on observational data and subject to human error, so please approach this with a healthy dose of skepticism.

BABIP (batting average on balls in play) is calculated using the same methodology as it is for position players, but it often tells us more about a pitcher than it does a hitter. With pitchers, a high BABIP is often due to poor defense or bad luck, and can often be an indicator of potential rebound, and a low BABIP may be cause to expect performance regression. (A typical league-average BABIP is close to .290-.300.)

After a witty 150ish words on the player like only Baseball Prospectus's staff can provide, it's on to that second stat block, which repeats the YEAR, TEAM, LVL, and AGE columns. The metrics **WHIP** (walks plus hits per inning pitched) and **ERA** (earned run average) are old standbys: WHIP measures walks and hits allowed on a per-inning basis, while ERA measures earned runs on a nine-inning basis. Neither of these stats are translated or adjusted.

DRA (Deserved Run Average) was described at length earlier, and measures how many runs the pitcher "deserved" to allow per nine innings. Please note that since we lack all the data points that would make for a "real" DRA for minor-league events, the DRA displayed for minor league partial-seasons is based off of different data. (That data is a modified version of our cFIP metric, which you can find more information about on our website.)

Jacob deGrom   RHP
Born: 06/19/88   Age: 31   Bats: L   Throws: R
Height: 6'4"   Weight: 180   Origin: Round 9, 2010 Draft (#272 overall)

YEAR	TEAM	LVL	AGE	W	L	SV	G	GS	IP	H	HR	BB/9	K/9	K	GB%	BABIP
2016	NYN	MLB	28	7	8	0	24	24	148	142	15	2.2	8.7	143	47%	.312
2017	NYN	MLB	29	15	10	0	31	31	201[1]	180	28	2.6	10.7	239	48%	.305
2018	NYN	MLB	30	10	9	0	32	32	217	152	10	1.9	11.2	269	48%	.281
2019	NYN	MLB	31	13	9	0	31	31	186	145	18	2.3	10.7	221	46%	.286

Breakout: 8%   Improve: 29%   Collapse: 28%   Attrition: 6%   MLB: 85%
Comparables: Erik Bedard, A.J. Burnett, CC Sabathia

YEAR	TEAM	LVL	AGE	WHIP	ERA	DRA	WARP	MPH	FB%	WHF	CSP
2016	NYN	MLB	28	1.20	3.04	3.30	3.5	96.3	59.6	12.1	47.2
2017	NYN	MLB	29	1.19	3.53	3.02	5.7	97.2	55.5	14.5	49.5
2018	NYN	MLB	30	0.91	1.70	2.09	8.0	98.2	52.1	16.3	48.4
2019	NYN	MLB	31	1.02	2.91	3.23	3.9	96.6	54.5	14.8	48.2

Just like with hitters, **WARP** (Wins Above Replacement Player) is a total value metric that puts pitchers of all stripes on the same scale as position players. We use DRA as the primary input for our calculation of WARP. You might notice that relief pitchers (due to their limited innings) may have a lower WARP than you were expecting or than you might see in other WARP-like metrics. WARP does not take leverage into account, just the actions a pitcher performs and the expected value of those actions ... which ends up judging high-leverage relief pitchers differently than you might imagine given their prestige and market value.

MPH gives you the pitcher's 95th percentile velocity for the noted season, in order to give you an idea of what the *peak* fastball velocity a pitcher possesses. Since this comes from our pitch tracking data, it is not publicly available for minor-league pitchers.

Finally, we display the three new pitching metrics we described earlier. **FB%** (fastball percentage) gives you the percentage of fastballs thrown out of all pitches. **WhiffRt** (whiff rate) tells you the percentage of swinging strikes induced out of all pitches. **CS Prob** (called strike probability) expresses the likelihood of all pitches thrown to result in a called strike, after controlling for factors like handedness, umpire, pitch type, count, and location.

PECOTA

All players have PECOTA projections for 2019, as well as a set of other numbers that describe the performance of comparable players according to PECOTA. All projections for 2019 are for the player at the date we went to press in early January and are projected into the league and park context as indicated by the team abbreviation. All PECOTA projected statistics represent a player's projected major-league performance.

The numbers beneath the player's stats–Breakout, Improve, Collapse, Attrition–are part and parcel of the PECOTA projections. They estimate the likelihood of changes in performance relative to the player's previously-established level of production, based on the performance of comparable players:

Breakout Rate is the percent change that a player's production will improve by at least 20 percent relative to the weighted average of his performance over his most recent seasons.

Improve Rate is the percent chance that a player's production will improve at all relative to his baseline performance. A player who is expected to perform just the same as he has in the recent past will have an Improve Rate of 50 percent.

Collapse Rate is the percent chance that a position player's production will decline by at least 25 percent relative to his baseline performance.

Attrition Rate operates on playing time rather than performance. Specifically, it measures the likelihood that a player's playing time will decrease by at least 50 percent relative to his established level.

Breakout Rate and Collapse Rate can sometimes be counterintuitive for players who have already experienced a radical change in performance level. It's also worth noting that the projected decline in a player's rate performances might not be indicative of an expected decline in underlying ability or skill, but could just be an anticipated correction following a breakout season.

MLB% is the percentage of similar players who played in the major leagues in their relevant season.

The final pieces of information are the player's three highest-scoring comparable players as determined by PECOTA. All comparables represent a snapshot of how the listed player was performing at the same age as the current player, so if a 23-year-old pitcher is compared to Bartolo Colon, he's actually being compared to a 23-year-old Colon, not the version that pitched for the Rangers in 2018, nor to Colon's career as a whole.

Chicago Cubs 2019

A few points about pitcher projections. First, we aren't yet projecting peak velocity, so that column will be blank in the PECOTA lines. Second, projecting DRA is trickier than evaluating past performance, because it is unclear how deserving each pitcher will be of his anticipated outcomes. However, we know that another DRA-related statistic–contextual FIP or cFIP–estimates future run scoring very well. So for PECOTA, the projected DRA figures you see are based on the past cFIPs generated by the pitcher and comparable players over time, along with the other factors described above.

Lineouts

In each chapter's Lineouts section, you'll find abbreviated text comments, as well as most of same information you'd find in our full player comments. We limit the stats boxes in this section to only including the 2018 information for each player.

Exclusive Player Visualizations

In our constant battle to provide you with new and interesting baseball content you can't find anywhere else, we've added a trio of data visualizations to each hitter's entry in these books and a pair of visualizations for each pitcher.

For hitters, you'll find three new infographics. The first is each player's **Batted Ball Distribution**, which displays the five major sections of the field: LF (left), LCF (left center), CF (center), RCF (right center), and RF (right). The percentage indicated tells us what percentage of batted balls from that hitter fell within that part of the field during the 2018 season. We've also included the hitter's slugging percentage on balls in play (also called **SLGCON**) for that part of the field.

You'll also see two heatmaps: **Strike Zone vs LHP** and **Strike Zone vs RHP**. These heat maps represent a view of the strike zone from behind the catcher. Areas where there is a darker coloration represent the places where a higher percentage of pitches resulted in hits. In other words, the heatmap represents a hitter's "sweet spots" for getting hits against either left-handed or right-handed pitchers, depending on the image.

Pitchers get two images that help explain what their pitches look like from a hitter's perspective: **Pitch Shape vs LHH** and **Pitch Shape vs RHH**. These images show you the shape and the "tunneling" effect of each pitcher's offerings from the batter's perspective. For each type of pitch that a pitcher throws (represented by an indicator shape), there's a set of dots indicating the flight path, where each dot represents a 0.01-second interval. This maps the average trajectory and speed of an offering, ending where the ball crosses the plate. The solid black box represents the regular strike zone, while the gray contour lines indicate the range of locations that a pitcher typically works in.

Below the image, we provide a bit more detailed information about each pitcher's average offering in the **Pitch Types** box. Here, we also list each of the pitcher's major offerings under the **Type** column.

- **Fastballs** (which usually refers to the four-seam variation)
- **Sinkers** and/or two-seam fastballs
- **Cutters** (which could include "hard" cutters like cut fastballs and "soft" cutters that resemble hard sliders)
- **Changeups** (not including most splitters)
- **Splitters** (split-fingered pitches, forkballs, and some split-changes)
- **Sliders** and/or slurves
- **Curveballs** (including spike-curveballs and knuckle-curveballs, as well as some slurvy curves)
- **Slow curveballs** and/or eephus pitches
- **Knuckleballs**
- **Screwballs**

The **Freq** column indicates the percentage of overall pitches that fall into each of those type categories; if a pitcher has a 16.55% score for changeups, then that's the percent of all pitches that he throws as changeups. **Velo** is exactly what you think it is: the average miles per hour for each pitch type. **H Mov** is the number of inches of horizontal movement on the average pitch of that type, while **V Mov** is the number of inches of vertical movement on the average pitch of that type. (At Baseball Prospectus, we measure this over the long flight of the ball and include gravity into the V Mov number in order to give you the most realistic representation of what the pitch *actually* does.)

If you're wondering about the second number in brackets, that's the index for that velocity or movement compared to the league average. Like DRC+, a score of 100 means that the speed or movement is about the same as league average, while a higher score means that there's higher velocity or movement than the league average. Numbers below 100 indicate less velocity or movement than the league average.

Part 1: Team Analysis

Table for Three: Previewing the 2019 Chicago Cubs

Josh Cole, Sam Fels and Zack Moser

ZACK MOSER: My first thought was to copy and paste last year's team preview in this space, since that appears to be the Cubs' roster construction strategy for 2019. My second thought was to copy and paste last year's preview in this space, but to make the text red so as to be a bit more menacing. But we must talk about the significantly-less-fun Cubs, and I'm glad that the three of us are tackling this thankless task.

At the risk of setting the (appropriately?) negative tone, what are your first thoughts about the 2019 Cubs? We can start with their schadenfreude-ian PECOTA projection of 79 wins, if you like.

SAM FELS: I feel like the text should have a little reaper emoji next to it, given the funeral shroud most of greater Cub-dom is walking around in these days.

I hate to argue with PECOTA, because it's just a projection, but this is still a team that cobbled 95 wins with barely half of Kris Bryant and no one other than Javier Báez even having above an average season for themselves. It's got a returning Yu Darvish as well, so while the lack of action in the winter has certainly been boring, and the quotes from ownership infuriating, it's hard for me to get too negative. Also, the PECOTA on Bryant is laughable, who's never been below a four-win player when healthy. I know I said I wouldn't….

JOSH COLE: Yeah—the doom and gloom is palpable. But I get it, to some extent. I mean, Bryce Harper posted this picture on Instagram of him, Bryant, and their wives all posing and smiling together, which many Cubs fans (definitely not me) took to mean that Harper was 100 percent, no questions asked, signing with the Cubs once he hit free agency. Now that ship has all but sailed, and I'm not sure I want to live in a world where I can't trust what I see on Instagram.

Ownership's insistence on thrift when the window for contention is closing and every team in the NL Central is adding valuable pieces (save the Pirates, it should go without saying) is puzzling, at best. I still get a little flutter every time I see the phrase "mystery team" linked to any of the remaining high-end free agents, but it's looking more and more like Cubs fans will have to be content with Brad Brach and Daniel Descalso as the big offseason splurges. What a time to be alive. Given some of the question marks with the team (which I'm sure we'll get into), 79 wins seems low, but certainly not unthinkable.

ZACK: I'm actually happy to defend the Bryant projection, with some caveats. Yes, Bryant has been an MVP-caliber player every year except 2018, but a 4.1 WARP projection with a 133 DRC+ is pretty damn good, and within the margin of error of other MVPs (Stanton, Yelich, Harper). There are only nine players pegged for five wins. Considering how PECOTA weighs recent contributions, I actually am a little surprised he isn't penalized more; his .272/.376/.473 projection is basically what he put up in 102 games last season. The slugging is what stands out, and I think a conservative outlook there is appropriate considering we don't know the status of his shoulder.

If there's one projection I can't get on board with, it's El Mago's—PECOTA isn't sold on his weird skill set (projected for a 108 DRC+ and 3.0 WARP), and neither are many analysts, but I think he's a good bet for a four-win year.

SAM: Yeah, Báez is weird. He carries what normally would be an unsustainable BABIP, but he hits the ball so hard that it's kind of normal for him. He's done it for three straight years. So while he might not put up quite the numbers of last year, he's still going to be a big contributor.

JOSH: Right. For me, Báez is a little like the hitter version of Kyle Hendricks in the sense that it would shock nobody if he beat his projections every year for the rest of his career. His style of play is so unpredictable that I'm not sure it can be captured by any projection system.

SAM: I think what PECOTA, and a lot of fans, are worrying about is the age of the pitching staff. Every starter save Kyle Hendricks is over 30, and he's 29. Jon Lester's decline may have started. Cole Hamels had a resurgence but we don't know if that's firmly in place now. José Quintana was up-and-down. Darvish is coming off an eight-start season. It's hard to predict stability for a rotation that's over 150 combined years old. On the plus side, the Cubs might have five number-two starters. On the bottom, they may not get a full season out of any of them and with four of them on the decline.

ZACK: You hit the nail on the head, Sam. Which makes the front office (or ownership's) reluctance to go after some impact arms for the bullpen all the more puzzling. Brach is a nice, low-risk add, and Pedro Strop and Steve Cishek are the workhorses. But with Brandon Morrow out to start the year and Carl Edwards Jr. taking a solid step back in 2018, this bullpen could put even more pressure on the ~~geezers~~ rotation to succeed.

If only the best closer of his generation were available for only money....

SAM: Y'know, I'm just not that worried about the bullpen. You can make a bullpen up on the fly if you have to. Again, there's a solid base there with Morrow (when and if healthy), Strop, Edwards, Cishek. Brach is fine, you'll find one or two others. There's always some tomato can who comes out of nowhere and strikes out 30% of the batters he sees for basically no reason. Let's just go with my guy Dillon Maples. One day he's going to be able to keep his fastball in the zip code.

JOSH: Maples! If you want to ride an emotional rollercoaster, read his 2018 Triple-A Iowa stat line left to right: the Hendricks-like 2.79 ERA is super exciting, as is the Kerry Wood-ian 17.5 strikeouts per nine. And then you see the Chatwood-esque 9.08 BB/9. But I'm with Sam: the stuff is clearly there for Maples, and if he can harness it, it would definitely be fun to watch him unleash that crazy slider in high-leverage spots.

Speaking of Chatwood, is it too soon to bring him up in this conversation?

ZACK: It's too soon.

JOSH: Chatwood fascinates me, because he's such a great example of how impossible baseball is to predict, even with the endless amount of data available. The spin rate, the home/road splits, getting away from Coors… it all pointed to unlocked potential. And yet… his 19.6 percent walk rate was seventh-highest of all time (min. 100 IP) and the highest since Mitch Williams (a guy whose nickname was literally "Wild Thing") in 1987. I can't recall a more frustrating Cubs player to watch since, I don't know… Milton Bradley? Is there any way the Cubs can salvage some value on the $25 million he's owed? Can he get it together enough to be a usable arm in the bullpen?

SAM: That's tricky. It obviously isn't a problem of stuff for Chatwood. He's got movement for days. He just can't get it anywhere near the plate. If he could even be somewhat controlled, he could be a real weapon. But that motion is just too herky-jerky to have consistent control.

ZACK: I think we've spent more time here talking about Chatwood than the Cubs themselves have talked about Chatwood's role on the 2019 team. I think he's as good as gone, either via trade or trebuchet.

SAM: Speaking of the rotation, here's another thing I think about, and tell me if I'm wrong. Another reason for the financial conservatism this year is that the Cubs are going to have to restock the rotation in the next two years and there's just not anything in the system that's going to be ready. Hamels will be off the team after this season. Lester and Quintana after next. Hendricks will come out of arbitration. At the very least the Cubs are going to have to fill in three rotation spots, and none of them are going to be cheap. Does that make sense?

ZACK: They definitely have a pitching problem on the horizon, but—like the many excuses before it—I think that line of thinking is more convenient cover for ownership than a driving force. So much money comes off the books in the next two to three years, so they should have no issues restocking the staff when they come to that crossroads. I think it's reason enough to say that making the best of this contention window is more important than worrying what to do when Lester *et al* depart. There will be a new CBA and likely new front office personnel by the time this team's window closes, and there's not enough talent in the pipeline to buoy legit contention past this window.

JOSH: Yeah—all along, the modus operandi of this front office has been to prioritize young hitters while cobbling together good enough starting pitching through trades and free agency, and they've done a reasonably good job at it, Chatwood notwithstanding (last Chatwood reference, I swear). I'm not worried about their willingness to shell out some money for starting pitching over the next few years; they won't have a choice.

Might as well keep the negativity rolling... I'm worried about Jon Lester over the next few years. By ERA alone, he was fine (3.32), but his 4.44 DRA tells a different story. His walks have risen in each of the past four years, and he saw a huge jump in contact (79.4 percent, up from 74.7 in 2017) and a huge dip in swings and misses (20.6 percent, down from 25.3 in 2017). He just didn't look like the same guy, and his stuff has deteriorated to the point that if his command is off even a bit, he gets rocked. I suppose he's crafty enough that his floor is probably a league average starter, which I suppose would be fine at the tail end of a six-year deal.

Do you guys see anyone in line for a collapse this year?

SAM: That's the thing with this team. I don't see a very low floor. Sure, Lester might not be what he's been, but you can't really see him being bad, can you? Maybe Quintana's 2018 is more the norm going forward, but he also could be considered the fifth starter? For a 4 or 5, that's pretty solid production. It's likely Báez isn't an MVP candidate again (in an admittedly down year for that particular race), but he's not going to be bad, either. Again, last year a lot of players on this team were at their "floor," and they won 95 games. It's easier to picture most of them being better than worse than last year. If I had to pick I would say Lester is a candidate but I don't expect it. Maybe Zobrist due to age, but it's unclear just how much he'll be used. And Jason Heyward is just a walking collapse.

ZACK: I agree that the Cubs would have to have exceptionally bad luck to be worse than their PECOTA projection. But I think that they've done the worst possible job keeping up with a restocked National League, across the board and in their division. They won 95 last year, but the teams they can beat up on just aren't as plentiful going into 2019. You're more optimistic than I am, Sam, and anything short of a blockbuster free agent splash or trade won't convince me otherwise.

Ultimately, this team's window might be slamming shut before our eyes because of some fierce anti-labor tactics, and not only does that rankle philosophically... it makes for boring baseball. Last year, I picked the team for 96 wins and they made good on that. This year, I can squint and see 90, but really anything between 80 and 95 seems possible, and the lower end is likely.

Considering the improvements in the division and NL, I'm compelled to be conservative and say 85-77.

JOSH: I see Kris Bryant rebounding, Anthony Rizzo hitting 25-30 homers and driving in 100 like he does every year, Javier Baez breaking projection systems the world over, and the pitching staff relying on guile and veteran savvy in order to push the Cubs into the Wild Card for the second straight year. I'll go with 90-72.

Performance Graphs

2018 Hit List Ranking

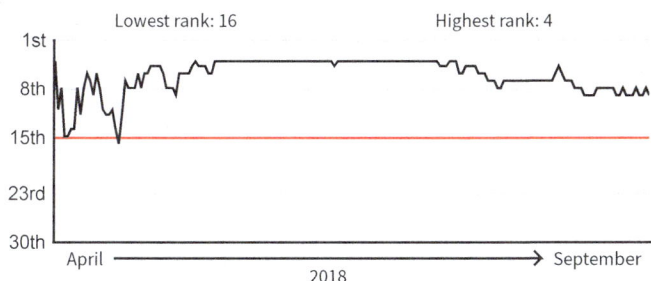

Committed Payroll (in millions)

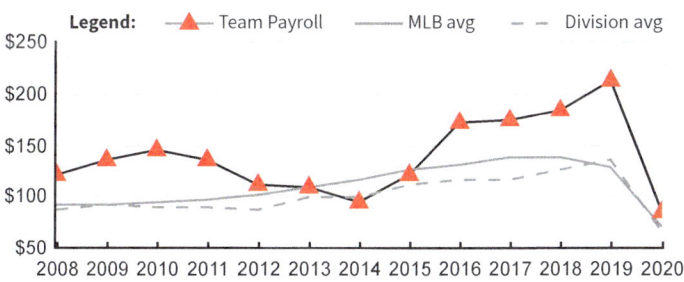

Farm System Ranking

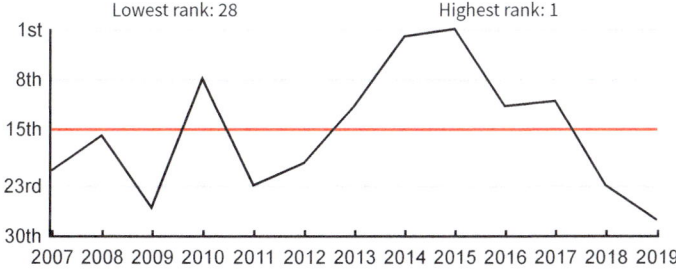

2018 Team Performance

ACTUAL STANDINGS

Team	W	L	Pct
MIL	96	67	.588
CHN	**95**	**68**	**.582**
SLN	88	74	.543
PIT	82	79	.509
CIN	67	95	.413

THIRD-ORDER STANDINGS

Team	W	L	Pct
MIL	93	70	.570
CHN	**92**	**71**	**.564**
SLN	83	79	.512
PIT	78	83	.484
CIN	71	91	.438

TOP HITTERS

Player	WARP
Javier Baez	4.6
Anthony Rizzo	4.1
Ben Zobrist	3.6

TOP PITCHERS

Player	WARP
Kyle Hendricks	5
Jen-Ho Tseng	2.6
Duane Underwood	2.4

VITAL STATISTICS

Statistic Name	Value	Rank
Pythagenpat	.576	7th
Runs Scored per Game	4.67	11th
Runs Allowed per Game	3.96	3rd
Deserved Runs Created Plus	94	18th
Deserved Run Average	4.57	20th
Fielding Independent Pitching	4.09	17th
Defensive Efficiency Rating	.715	6th
Batter Age	27.0	4th
Pitcher Age	30.0	27th
Salary	$183.2M	4th
Marginal $ per Marginal Win	$3.7M	18th
Disabled List Days	$906.0M	8th
$ on DL	19%	20th

2019 Team Projections

PROJECTED STANDINGS

Team	W	L	Pct	+/-
MIL	88	74	.543	-8
SLN	85	77	.524	-3
CIN	81	81	.500	+14
PIT	80	82	.493	-2
CHN	79	83	.487	-16

TOP PROJECTED HITTERS

Player	WARP
Anthony Rizzo	4.8
Kris Bryant	3.9
Javier Baez	3.0

TOP PROJECTED PITCHERS

Player	WARP
Kyle Hendricks	1.8
Yu Darvish	1.7
Jose Quintana	1.7

FARM SYSTEM REPORT

Top Prospect	Number of Top 101 Prospects
Nico Hoerner, #86	1

KEY DEDUCTIONS

Player	WARP
Daniel Murphy	4.0
Justin Wilson	0.3

KEY ADDITIONS

Player	WARP
Kendall Graveman	0.5
Daniel Descalso	0.3

Team Personnel

President
Theo Epstein

General Manager
Jed Hoyer

Senior Vice President
Jason McLeod

Assistant General Manager
Scott Harris

Assistant General Manager
Randy Bush

Manager
Joe Maddon

BP Alumni
Bryan Cole
Jeremy Greenhouse

Wrigley Field Stats

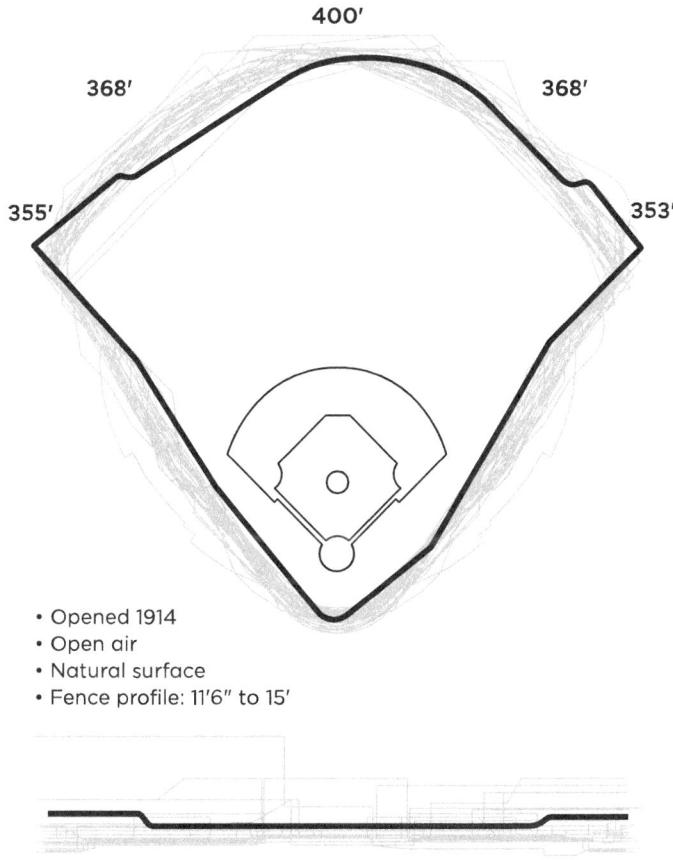

- Opened 1914
- Open air
- Natural surface
- Fence profile: 11'6" to 15'

Three-Year Park Factors

Runs	Runs/RH	Runs/LH	HR/RH	HR/LH
102	104	98	104	90

Cubs Team Analysis

"Who led the Cubs in home runs two years ago?" asked Dad, shifting from second to third as we cleared the rickety, rust-riddled bridge over Aux Sable Creek. Our Suburban barreled on as the gravel dust it kicked up settled gently onto the fully matured corn leaves in the fields lining the road. We lived amongst the corn and soybean fields outside of Minooka, Illinois—the 50 miles separating it from Chicago felt more like 50 years. Rural life, it turns out, especially in decades past, was a great setting for baseball.

"1982? 'Bull' Durham. Twenty-two homers." answered my sister with a sigh, disappointed by any question that didn't refer to her heart's lifelong obsession, catcher Jody Davis.

I, for one, was relieved that Laurie had once again beaten me to the punch, as my guess was going to be everybody's favorite first baseman, Bill Buckner. I have always been prone to follow my heart more than my brain, but I mean, come on, black mitt, black cleats and a push-broom mustache? Badass. He may have later acquired fame of another shade in Boston, but in our town and at that time, Buckner was the bomb. All of that favorable evidence was notwithstanding, however, as he was the wrong answer to Dad's question.

On these frequent occasions when he would drive me and my sister home after school or baseball practice, we reveled in our Dad's invocation of the Cubby questions. Our lives were wonderfully less distracted then, before the internet and smartphones so completely usurped our collective attention. We (mostly) worked as required at school, sports and band, and then hungrily filled the remainder of our spare time and brain-pan real estate with the minutiae of the Cubs season and roster (ok, and some Dungeons and Dragons on my part, and Duran Duran on Laurie's…and maybe mine too. If you can't admit that John Taylor was and is a beautiful specimen then I declare that you are not in touch with your inner mammal).

Mom's team was the Cubs and Dad's team was the Cubs, so by God our team became the Cubs. Aunts, uncles, grandparents, cousins and pets: it was most assuredly in our blood. We were born breathers of oxygen, consumers of buttered sweet corn, drinkers of beer, players of Liverpool Rummy and mowers of grass, but above all we were born die-hard Cubs fans.

Our birthright indoctrination into Cubs fandom was not so much a conscious choice on the part of our folks as merely a continuation in the tradition of survival economy that is so imperative in farming families. We were taught to follow

Chicago Cubs 2019

our charismatic baseball team in the same way we were instructed to garden, cook, sew, read, hammer and use good manners. It mattered not at all to us that the Cubs were the butt of every MLB rejoinder; famously ill-fated to forever fail, unfairly goat-cursed to never win another World Series, or to even get close.

Our fandom was unflappable. It was not to be flapped. Like anybody's hometown team, the Cubs were quite simply our fighting lads, and we gave them our adoration without question. Around 1978 or so, as I was playing with my G.I. Joe, the names I heard the announcers repeat on television or the radio began to stick and I began to wonder about these fellows. Buckner, Manny Trillo, Rick Reuschel, Bruce Sutter…but especially Trillo, who just sounded super-heroic in some way. When these names were broadcast, the specific attention that Dad would pay them made us pay attention, and thus we were hooked.

Baseball was a way of life in the Offerman household. Despite his ever-burgeoning work schedule, our Dad also found time to play catch, hit us grounders and coach us—throwing us "major-league pop-ups" that seemed to ascend until they gently smooched the very clouds before plummeting back down towards our eager, outstretched mitts. ("No, no. Let the ball come to you. Then give.") He understood fundamentals as a way of life and he patiently taught that to us in every possible instance. Mentally and physically, we learned that any success is merely a series of properly executed events strung together without dropping the ball, as it were. When Dad said "keep your eye on the ball; watch it all the way to the bat," we knew this could be applied to not only our actual hitting technique, but also metaphorically to life in general. Mom and Dad both were great adherents of the idea that in order to become better than oneself, a great deal of obstinate practice was required. You didn't just hit a home run or bake a perfect loaf of bread on the first try. You had to put your head down and work at it.

From the late seventies through the eighties, the Cubs generally had a scrappy good time of it, and we cheered them on like their lives depended on our scrutiny. Our front yard was about an acre and a half, and Laurie and I would drive the family tractor mower in simple laps from the house out to the road and back again. We learned to take turns of three laps each, while the other sibling would simultaneously watch the game in the living room and the progress of the mower out the window. Of course, we got good enough at it that we barely needed to stop the tractor when switching off every seven minutes or so, shouting any game developments to each other. Our enthusiasm was entirely unaffected by the fact that the Cubbies finished well below .500 in ten of the 12 years I was in the Minooka School System. Besides, when a team has had such thrilling MVP players in every era, like Ernie Banks, Ryne Sandberg, Rick Sutcliffe, Mark Grace, Sammy Sosa, Fergie Jenkins, Billy Williams, Kerry Wood, Andre Dawson, Dave Kingman, Greg Maddux and Leon Durham, to name but a handful, it never felt like we were backing a team of losers regardless of the scoreboard.

It also doesn't hurt that the team talent and fan solidarity are intensely displayed in the crucible of the nation's greatest ballpark, Wrigley Field. My earliest memory is from 1980 or so, and the eldritch-seeming riveted steel girders comprising the skeleton of the stadium's innards with its wide ramp walkways and main concourse of souvenir stands, hot dogs, pretzels and beer taps. It was as magnificent to us as any pyramid Giza could provide. Emerging from the beehive of concessions below to the sunshine illuminating the cerulean sky, green outfield grass and ivy on the brick walls lent an immediate magic to the proceedings. Our annual trip to the "Friendly Confines" became an absolute highlight of the summer, and not just because our folks made sure to take us on a giveaway day. Jersey Day was my favorite—the greatest shirt of my youth was a three-quarters-sleeve jersey with a large Cubs logo on the front and a Keebler Elf-in-his-tree advertisement on the back.

Over the years, our familial attention spans have waxed and waned, but our fandom has burned true throughout. Our cheering section added two younger siblings, Matt and Carrie, who will forever hold a torch for Mark Grace and with good reason. Of all the teams in all the professional sports in the country, the Cubs have remained our household's only true love and we perhaps even began to take them a bit for granted in adulthood. That is, of course, until 2015. Thanks to a substantial rebuild, the Cubs were suddenly a contender in a way that we had not known in our lifetimes, and it's had a wonderfully rejuvenating effect on the world at large for Cubs fans. When they did break the curse (finally!) and win the World Series in 2016, the sensation was exquisitely climactic. If the ultimate sporting/sexual experience is achieved by the immense accumulation of tension due to incessant cycles of anticipation—arousal and denial, year after year, for *one hundred and eight years*—then the Cubs 2016 championship would have to unquestionably register as the greatest baseball orgasm in modern history.

These contemporary sluggers engender adoration in a substantial way that is based upon their actual league-leading performances, rather than just the handsome way they fill out their respective uniforms. Gold Glover Anthony Rizzo at first base is as dependable as a mountain, and he is also a flat-out hero when it comes to his generosity in charity work, specifically in the fight against cancer. The sense of moral character he displays, always with an easy smile, is all one could ever ask of a sports figure. Kris Bryant will likely bring his bat back to bear in the coming year, and he will be joined by fellow farm-raised standouts Kyle Schwarber, Albert Almora, Ian Happ and David Bote. All very exciting players who will dazzle you with their gloves and their wheels whilst only in their mid-twenties, which means they are only just beginning to realize their full potential on offense. And behind the plate, Wilson Contreras has developed the reputation of a very persnickety sheriff with his quick-draw talent for cutting down attempted base-stealers, as well as picking off dirty varmint runners with a lead he doesn't appreciate.

Chicago Cubs 2019

In baseball, winning requires talent and strategy, but timing and luck cannot be discounted (you also want to stay on the right side of any billy goat owners who might be attending the game). When the timing is right, the Cubs' starting rotation has the potential to be extremely dominant, depending upon the health of Yu Darvish or the couple of solid fellows available to take up his slack alongside Jon Lester, Kyle Hendricks, Jose Quintana and Cole Hamels. All four of these heartbreakers are more likely than not to befuddle opposing hitters, and they generally give off a sense of confidence going into their respective games. There is formidable strength in the bullpen as well, even with Brandon Morrow's uncertain future, and they score major bonus points for launching into a funky dance break every time a Cubs home run clears the fence.

With immense relish, this brings me to Javy Baez. Not since Sandberg's explosive MVP season of 1984 has a Cubs player provided such a consistent menu of delights to his disciples. His electricity at the plate is undeniable, his fielding is perhaps the best in the majors and the temerity with which he runs the bases is about as fun to watch as a Buster Keaton stunt. So physically impossible do his feats seem, particularly with regard to his defensive range, his cannon of an arm and his ability to literally tag base runners without even looking at them, that he has come to be nicknamed "El Mago," which means "The Magician."

Still, despite the immense triumph-tsunami manifested from the release of decades of dejection, the funny thing is that Wrigley Field doesn't feel terribly different to me today than it has over the years. Now that I am technically an adult, the ballpark doesn't feel quite so enormous or overwhelming. I am much more likely to raise an eyebrow at the price of a beer. Sometimes I get to throw out the first pitch or sing during the seventh-inning stretch, which I can only perhaps liken to the golden ticket that Charlie receives from Willy Wonka, especially because the view from the announcer's booth feels like you're floating above the park in a glass elevator.

It was magical then, as it is magical today, because it is the home of the Cubs. My family attendance has swelled to 24 souls in the seats—so substantial a group that we rent a bus to take us to the games. We have sat through two games in the last two seasons, both in rain, with a chill touching the upper forties, watching two underwhelming losses to mediocre teams, and we had the greatest time you could imagine. We're proper Midwesterners, so just the sheer sense of victory derived from consuming a bratwurst and a beer beneath a flimsy poncho without spoiling the bun is an accomplishment worthy of stoic celebration.

Only in hindsight do I realize that our family's deep enjoyment of the Cubs has to do with our adherence to the old saw, "it's not whether you win or lose, it's how you play the game." We love to track these particular north-side-of-Chicago players as their seasonal fortunes ebb and flow, so the number in the W column doesn't hold us in thrall nearly as much as the individual achievements of the players. All the tallies are a savory part of the meal—some for their rising, some for the opposite. We are equally impressed by "Wow, Jake Arrieta struck out nine today" and "Hey, Dad, Shawon Dunston struck out nine times in a double header!"

In eras past, the team has fielded pretty fun, but usually hit-or-miss, rosters with a few bright spots. What gives our family a new, warm feeling of confidence is this new idea wherein every position is manned by a fellow who might bring fireworks to the park on any given day. Our fortunes will undoubtedly wax and wane in the coming years, as they must, and the roster will turn over, as it will, but the lineup of Offermans will continue to grow and put up consistently impressive numbers as we cheer on our north-side boys. With so much talent and personality to fascinate me and my family, this Cubs team will undoubtedly see us arguing over who is the cutest, fastest and most exciting player for years to come, and that is good news to this fan of gardening.

Postscript: In Hollywood, a rather inordinate percentage of Chicago actors have found success amongst a very competitive talent pool comprised of performers from all over the world. I have often been asked why I think this might be, and the clear answer now occurs to me: the vast majority of these male and female thespians were raised as Cubs fans, which means that they have been inculcated with an unparalleled stubbornness; a tenacity which is perhaps required above all other qualities to succeed in Tinsel Town.

—Nick Offerman is an actor, writer and woodworker in Los Angeles.

Part 2: Player Analysis

Chicago Cubs 2019

Albert Almora CF
Born: 04/16/94 Age: 25 Bats: R Throws: R
Height: 6'2" Weight: 190 Origin: Round 1, 2012 Draft (#6 overall)

YEAR	TEAM	LVL	AGE	PA	R	2B	3B	HR	RBI	BB	K	SB	CS	AVG/OBP/SLG
2016	IOW	AAA	22	336	46	18	3	4	43	9	44	10	3	.303/.317/.416
2016	CHN	MLB	22	117	14	9	1	3	14	5	20	0	0	.277/.308/.455
2017	CHN	MLB	23	323	39	18	1	8	46	19	53	1	0	.298/.338/.445
2018	CHN	MLB	24	479	62	24	1	5	41	24	83	1	3	.286/.323/.378
2019	CHN	MLB	25	409	40	19	2	8	43	24	72	2	1	.268/.315/.393

Breakout: 7% Improve: 59% Collapse: 10% Attrition: 7% MLB: 98%
Comparables: Odubel Herrera, Jacoby Ellsbury, Billy Hamilton

Almora appeared in all but 11 Cubs games in 2018. He also started just 94 of them. No other player who appeared in at least 150 games was in the starting lineup for fewer than 125. In fact, only four other players in major league history have appeared in as many games in a single season without reaching 100 starts: early-career Shane Victorino and Andruw Jones, late-career Ichiro, and journeyman Jim Eisenreich. It's an unusual group, reflecting Almora's atypical role. He is something more than a fourth outfielder—fourth outfielders don't get almost 500 plate appearances—yet clearly short of a full-time regular. That's at least partly due to Joe Maddon's managerial tendencies and Chicago's roster construction. It's also an indication that Almora has not forced the issue with his performance. While evaluators and fans might talk about his glove as though he is an outfielder of Jones' caliber, the metrics do not agree, and he has yet to perform with the bat at a level that warrants 150 starts on a contender. Using Almora as a combination of fringe-average starter, platoon bat and defensive replacement is not inherently a problem for the team, but if he is to become a true full-time player, either his skills or his situation must change.

YEAR	TEAM	LVL	AGE	PA	DRC+	VORP	BABIP	BRR	FRAA	WARP
2016	IOW	AAA	22	336	106	22.5	.336	3.8	CF(69): -0.5, LF(6): 1.5	1.2
2016	CHN	MLB	22	117	92	5.2	.315	0.9	CF(33): -0.1, LF(8): 1.7	0.5
2017	CHN	MLB	23	323	93	15.9	.338	3.2	CF(104): -1.1, RF(1): 0.0	1.0
2018	CHN	MLB	24	479	85	10.7	.337	-0.1	CF(137): 2.5, LF(2): -0.1	1.0
2019	CHN	MLB	25	409	88	12.0	.307	-0.7	CF 0	0.9

Albert Almora, continued

Batted Ball Distribution

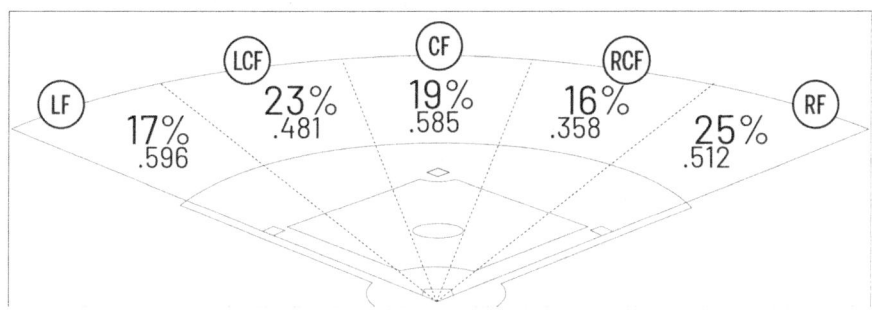

Strike Zone vs LHP

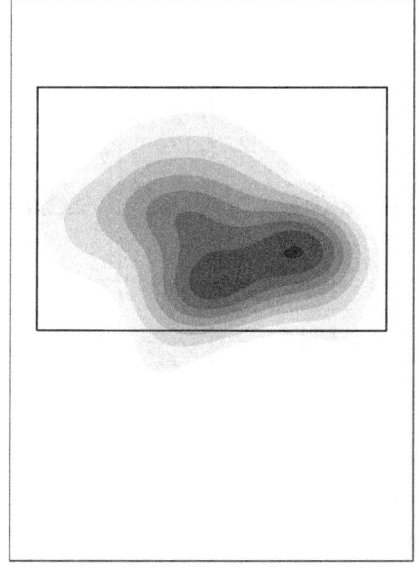

Strike Zone vs RHP

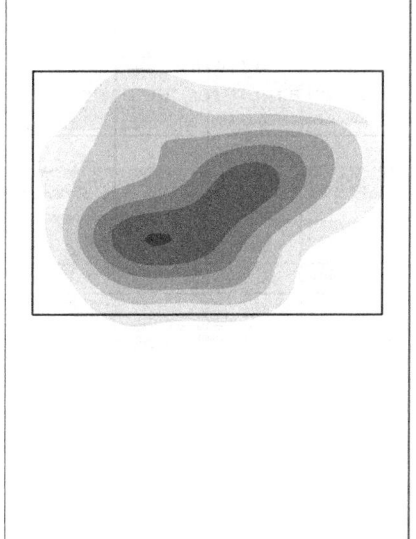

Javier Baez INF

Born: 12/01/92 Age: 26 Bats: R Throws: R
Height: 6'0" Weight: 190 Origin: Round 1, 2011 Draft (#9 overall)

YEAR	TEAM	LVL	AGE	PA	R	2B	3B	HR	RBI	BB	K	SB	CS	AVG/OBP/SLG
2016	CHN	MLB	23	450	50	19	1	14	59	15	108	12	3	.273/.314/.423
2017	CHN	MLB	24	508	75	24	2	23	75	30	144	10	3	.273/.317/.480
2018	CHN	MLB	25	645	101	40	9	34	111	29	167	21	9	.290/.326/.554
2019	CHN	MLB	26	662	97	30	6	27	80	45	172	19	7	.267/.322/.470

Breakout: 8% Improve: 52% Collapse: 11% Attrition: 12% MLB: 98%
Comparables: Danny Espinosa, Howie Kendrick, Starling Marte

As soon as he arrived in the majors, Baez exuded talent in almost every facet of the game, from his prodigious bat speed to the outrageous flair of his glovework and a swim move that even Michael Phelps would envy. One issue seemed to be holding him back from becoming truly elite: patience. If Baez could just learn a little more restraint at the right time, surely he would join the game's elite. Instead, Baez did the opposite: he swung more than almost anyone in baseball, had one of the league's worst contact rates, and still became a legitimate MVP candidate. Mechanical changes, like moving his hands away from his body and adding a higher leg kick, have helped the Puerto Rico native make quality contact on a more regular basis, transforming him from the league's most spectacular average player into the star that his talent always promised.

YEAR	TEAM	LVL	AGE	PA	DRC+	VORP	BABIP	BRR	FRAA	WARP
2016	CHN	MLB	23	450	90	20.2	.336	-0.7	3B(62): 1.1, 2B(59): 2.7	1.3
2017	CHN	MLB	24	508	94	30.0	.345	4.4	2B(80): -1.3, SS(73): -6.6	1.3
2018	CHN	MLB	25	645	120	54.7	.347	3.2	2B(104): -0.6, SS(65): 1.3	4.6
2019	CHN	MLB	26	662	108	33.6	.327	1.5	SS -1, 2B -1	3.0

Javier Baez, continued

Batted Ball Distribution

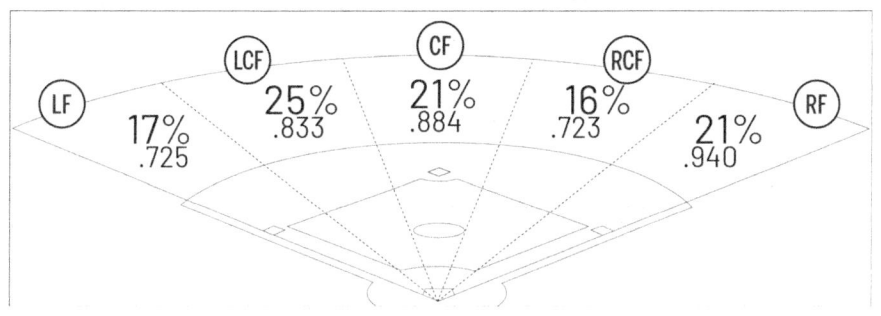

Strike Zone vs LHP   **Strike Zone vs RHP**

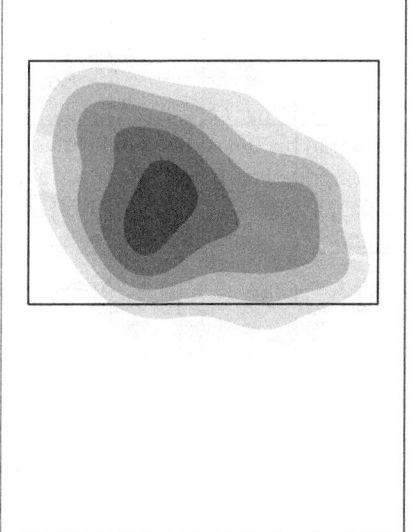

David Bote UT

Born: 04/07/93 Age: 26 Bats: R Throws: R
Height: 6'1" Weight: 210 Origin: Round 18, 2012 Draft (#554 overall)

YEAR	TEAM	LVL	AGE	PA	R	2B	3B	HR	RBI	BB	K	SB	CS	AVG/OBP/SLG
2016	TEN	AA	23	27	1	0	0	0	1	2	6	0	0	.200/.259/.200
2016	MYR	A+	23	313	55	26	3	6	41	31	41	6	1	.337/.410/.518
2017	TEN	AA	24	536	65	30	3	14	59	49	101	5	2	.272/.353/.438
2018	IOW	AAA	25	263	34	10	2	13	41	26	63	3	1	.268/.342/.494
2018	CHN	MLB	25	210	23	9	2	6	33	19	60	3	4	.239/.319/.408
2019	CHN	MLB	26	209	25	7	1	8	25	19	58	2	1	.226/.303/.403

Breakout: 12% Improve: 44% Collapse: 12% Attrition: 29% MLB: 74%
Comparables: Todd Frazier, Brendan Harris, Rob Refsnyder

Get your towels ready, it's about to go down. There was a point in 2018 when it felt like Bote was finishing more games than most closers. He produced one of the most memorable moments of the season when he hit a walk-off grand slam in a 4-3 win over the Nationals in August. It was Bote's second walk-off of the season, rather more iconic than his walk-off walk in early July. Two weeks after the slam, he hit another game-ending blast, cementing his status as late-inning hero and ensuring that anyone who didn't already know how to pronounce his name would get the memo (it's Bow-dee, not Boaty or Boat, much to T-Pain's chagrin). Far less secure is a regular role going forward. Bote clearly has a ton of thunder in his bat, but his defensive utility is up for debate and beyond the heroics, the overall offensive production was simply average after he slumped in the final six weeks. That's not likely to get him on that big, blue watery road to regular playing time, no matter how many walk-offs he produces.

YEAR	TEAM	LVL	AGE	PA	DRC+	VORP	BABIP	BRR	FRAA	WARP
2016	TEN	AA	23	27	58	-1.9	.263	0.2	3B(5): 0.3, 1B(2): 0.1	0.0
2016	MYR	A+	23	313	182	39.6	.378	1.5	2B(31): -2.1, 3B(21): 0.7	2.5
2017	TEN	AA	24	536	121	31.2	.318	1.0	2B(107): 5.7, RF(9): 1.2	2.4
2018	IOW	AAA	25	263	129	16.4	.313	-0.2	2B(38): -2.9, SS(15): 1.3	1.3
2018	CHN	MLB	25	210	77	7.3	.314	-1.0	3B(56): 2.4, 2B(13): -0.6	0.2
2019	CHN	MLB	26	209	91	4.0	.287	-0.2	3B 0, 2B 0	0.4

David Bote, continued

Batted Ball Distribution

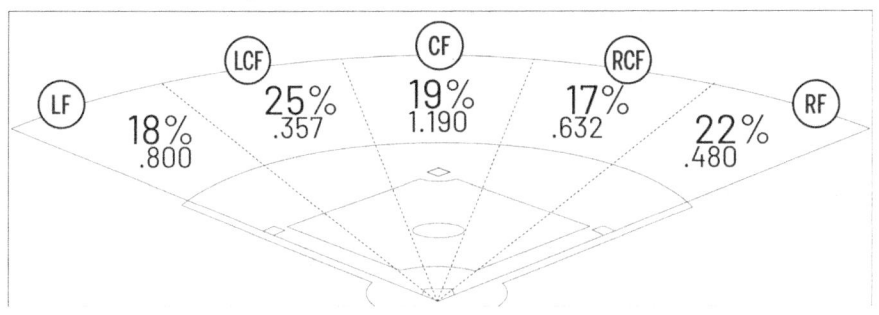

Strike Zone vs LHP **Strike Zone vs RHP**

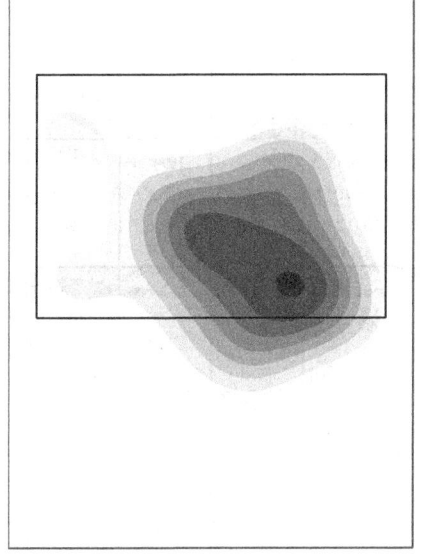

Chicago Cubs 2019

Kris Bryant 3B
Born: 01/04/92   Age: 27   Bats: R   Throws: R
Height: 6'5"   Weight: 230   Origin: Round 1, 2013 Draft (#2 overall)

YEAR	TEAM	LVL	AGE	PA	R	2B	3B	HR	RBI	BB	K	SB	CS	AVG/OBP/SLG
2016	CHN	MLB	24	699	121	35	3	39	102	75	154	8	5	.292/.385/.554
2017	CHN	MLB	25	665	111	38	4	29	73	95	128	7	5	.295/.409/.537
2018	CHN	MLB	26	457	59	28	3	13	52	48	107	2	4	.272/.374/.460
2019	CHN	MLB	27	621	81	32	3	22	82	74	134	6	4	.271/.374/.468

Breakout: 2%   Improve: 53%   Collapse: 12%   Attrition: 3%   MLB: 99%
Comparables: Evan Longoria, David Wright, Bob Horner

As Bryant goes, so do the Cubs. A stellar rookie campaign ended the franchise's six-year playoff drought, though his near 200 strikeouts foreshadowed an NLCS in which the team was blown away by Mets pitching. The triumphant MVP season followed, with a now 25-year-old Bryant leading Chicago to that historic World Series title. 2017 proved more challenging, as he battled through a hand injury. The team won the division comfortably in the end and Bryant, while diminished, was still one of the league's best players, but they both fell flat in the NLCS. 2018 was the team's most disappointing year since Bryant's debut, as shoulder inflammation limited him to 102 games and sapped his power when he was in the lineup. Just one more win would have ensured the division, a win their star third baseman would surely have provided if healthy. Instead the Cubs lost the division and then the Wild Card game. Theo Epstein and company probably didn't quite have this level of dependence in mind when they were building their franchise around Bryant.

YEAR	TEAM	LVL	AGE	PA	DRC+	VORP	BABIP	BRR	FRAA	WARP
2016	CHN	MLB	24	699	140	86.5	.332	3.4	3B(107): 1.5, LF(60): 1.1	6.1
2017	CHN	MLB	25	665	137	69.6	.334	1.9	3B(144): -3.9, RF(7): 0.2	5.3
2018	CHN	MLB	26	457	109	31.3	.342	-2.2	3B(86): 0.8, RF(15): 0.0	1.9
2019	CHN	MLB	27	621	131	40.5	.324	-1.1	3B 1, LF 0	3.9

Kris Bryant, continued

Batted Ball Distribution

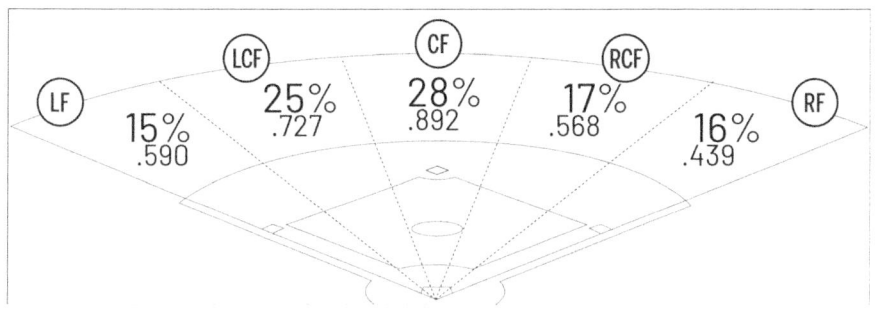

Strike Zone vs LHP

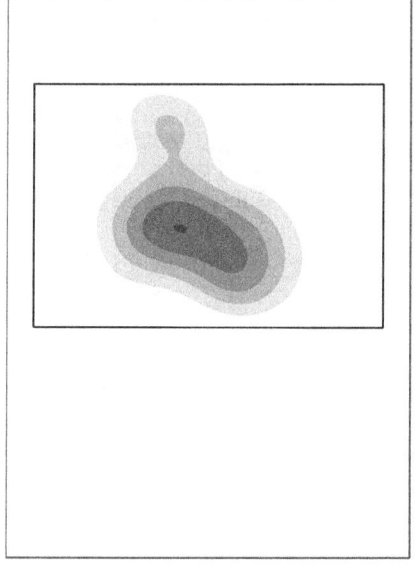

Strike Zone vs RHP

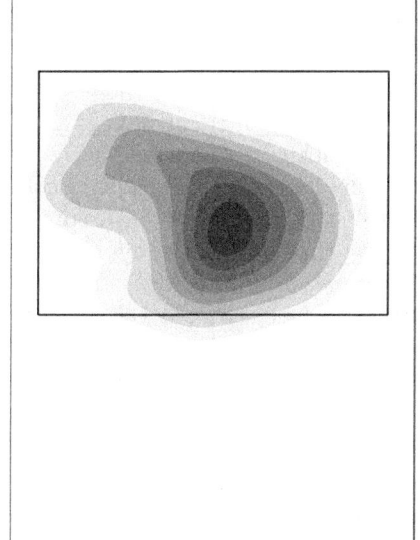

Chicago Cubs 2019

Victor Caratini C

Born: 08/17/93 Age: 25 Bats: B Throws: R
Height: 6'1" Weight: 215 Origin: Round 2, 2013 Draft (#65 overall)

YEAR	TEAM	LVL	AGE	PA	R	2B	3B	HR	RBI	BB	K	SB	CS	AVG/OBP/SLG
2016	TEN	AA	22	480	57	25	2	6	47	54	80	2	1	.291/.375/.405
2017	IOW	AAA	23	326	50	27	3	10	61	27	48	1	0	.342/.393/.558
2017	CHN	MLB	23	66	6	3	0	1	2	4	13	0	0	.254/.333/.356
2018	IOW	AAA	24	137	13	7	0	4	22	18	25	0	0	.313/.409/.478
2018	CHN	MLB	24	200	21	7	0	2	21	12	42	0	0	.232/.293/.304
2019	CHN	MLB	25	234	25	13	1	6	28	19	49	0	0	.262/.326/.419

Breakout: 8% Improve: 53% Collapse: 7% Attrition: 27% MLB: 85%
Comparables: Hank Conger, J.R. Towles, Jonathan Lucroy

YEAR	TEAM	P. COUNT	FRM RUNS	BLK RUNS	THRW RUNS	TOT RUNS
2017	CHN	1182	-1.0	0.5	0.0	-0.6
2017	IOW	7230	-3.9	0.6	0.1	-3.6
2018	CHN	4929	-1.0	0.3	0.1	-1.1
2018	IOW	2828	-1.9	0.0	-0.1	-1.5
2019	CHN	4987	-3.3	0.3	-0.2	-3.2

Is Caratini a supporting cast member who never gets promoted to regular, or will he get a chance to play lead? After nearly 500 plate appearances of impressive offense in Triple-A, he was called upon to backup Willson Contreras and stretch out at a corner infield spot when needed. Unfortunately, American Airlines lost his bat on the 90-minute sojourn to Chicago. Instead of an above-average hitter who warranted that quasi-utility role but had some big questions behind the plate, the Cubs got passable defense and the worst offensive production of any player on the team by some margin. There are many ways to be a "tweener," and Caratini now fits multiple definitions of the term, but his flexibility and track record in the minors will give him more chances to shed all forms of that label.

YEAR	TEAM	LVL	AGE	PA	DRC+	VORP	BABIP	BRR	FRAA	WARP
2016	TEN	AA	22	480	136	29.3	.341	-1.5	C(82): -9.0, 1B(30): -0.1	1.5
2017	IOW	AAA	23	326	146	34.4	.375	1.4	C(50): -3.9, 1B(30): 0.7	2.3
2017	CHN	MLB	23	66	76	0.5	.311	-0.4	C(12): -0.6, 1B(8): 0.1	-0.1
2018	IOW	AAA	24	137	139	12.2	.364	-0.6	C(18): -2.2, 1B(12): 1.6	0.8
2018	CHN	MLB	24	200	70	-1.4	.290	-0.6	C(37): -0.8, 1B(20): 0.5	0.0
2019	CHN	MLB	25	234	104	9.6	.316	-0.4	C -4, 1B 0	0.5

Victor Caratini, continued

Batted Ball Distribution

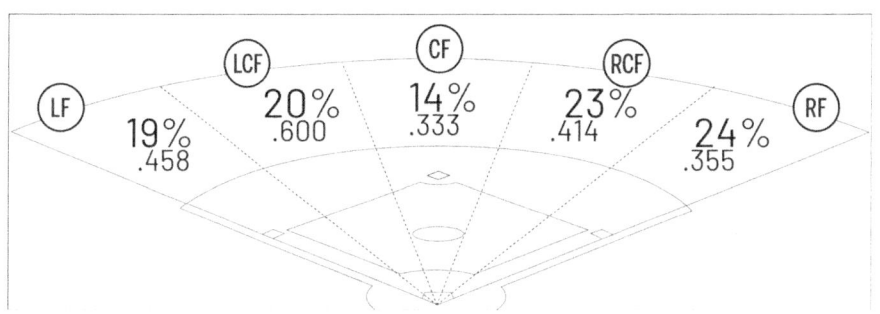

Strike Zone vs LHP

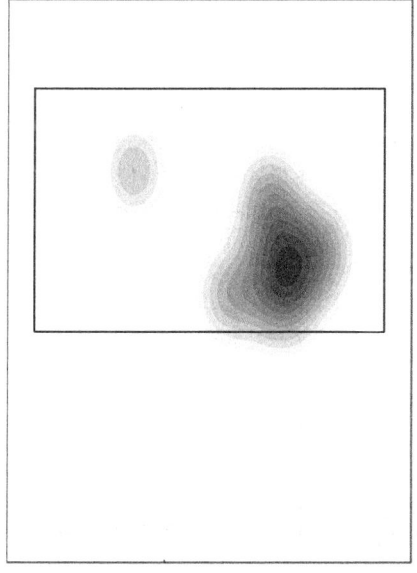

Strike Zone vs RHP

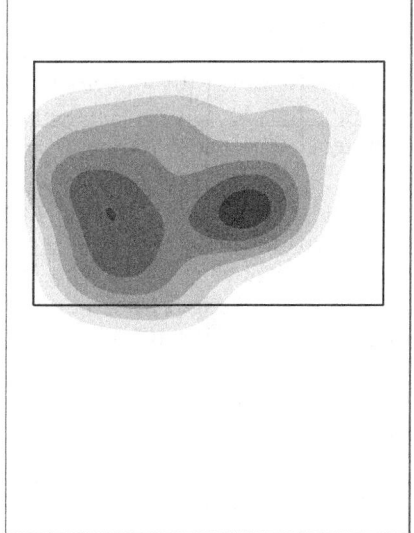

Chicago Cubs 2019

Willson Contreras   C

Born: 05/13/92   Age: 27   Bats: R   Throws: R
Height: 6'1"   Weight: 210   Origin: International Free Agent, 2009

YEAR	TEAM	LVL	AGE	PA	R	2B	3B	HR	RBI	BB	K	SB	CS	AVG/OBP/SLG
2016	IOW	AAA	24	240	40	16	3	9	43	28	32	4	4	.353/.442/.593
2016	CHN	MLB	24	283	33	14	1	12	35	26	67	2	2	.282/.357/.488
2017	CHN	MLB	25	428	50	21	0	21	74	45	98	5	4	.276/.356/.499
2018	CHN	MLB	26	544	50	27	5	10	54	53	121	4	1	.249/.339/.390
2019	CHN	MLB	27	514	59	22	3	15	61	52	114	5	3	.251/.337/.412

Breakout: 3%   Improve: 52%   Collapse: 14%   Attrition: 6%   MLB: 99%
Comparables: Derek Norris, Wil Myers, Carlos Santana

YEAR	TEAM	P. COUNT	FRM RUNS	BLK RUNS	THRW RUNS	TOT RUNS
2016	CHN	6569	5.0	1.4	0.8	7.6
2017	CHN	14005	-2.8	0.6	-1.1	-1.1
2018	CHN	18508	-17.8	1.9	0.4	-15.0
2019	CHN	17482	-11.6	1.7	0.0	-10.0

Contreras is one of the game's best backstops in a variety of ways. He caught 34 percent of attempted base stealers and picked off another seven runners, more than any other catcher in the majors. He's also one of the game's best blockers, ranking in the top five in Blocking Runs. There's just one issue: his presentation is worse than those PowerPoints with 50-word bullet points and completely incongruent animation that Jordan from Marketing makes you sit through in the team meetings every Monday morning. Contreras cost his team dearly with his framing this year, negating all the runs he gained in the other defensive areas and then some. Add to that a relative power outage that Chili Davis is probably blaming on millennials right now and it wasn't quite the progression one might expect from a 26-year-old. Framing hasn't been such a big issue in the past, and it's possible that fatigue from playing in so many games cost him with both bat and glove. In fact, his 1,109 innings caught in 2018 were over 70 more than the next most used backstop. If MLB ever considers introducing an automated strike zone, Contreras should be leading the campaign, as it might make him the game's best overall catcher.

YEAR	TEAM	LVL	AGE	PA	DRC+	VORP	BABIP	BRR	FRAA	WARP
2016	IOW	AAA	24	240	188	38.1	.382	-0.9	C(45): -4.5	2.3
2016	CHN	MLB	24	283	104	21.5	.339	-0.9	C(57): 6.7, LF(24): -2.5	1.6
2017	CHN	MLB	25	428	116	34.2	.319	-3.9	C(108): 0.7, 1B(5): 0.0	2.6
2018	CHN	MLB	26	544	90	27.0	.313	0.6	C(133): -14.6, LF(5): -0.8	0.5
2019	CHN	MLB	27	514	105	25.6	.304	-0.5	C -11	1.4

Willson Contreras, continued

Batted Ball Distribution

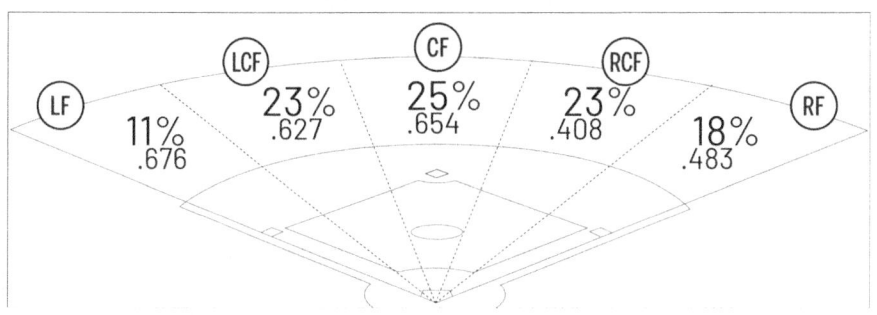

Strike Zone vs LHP

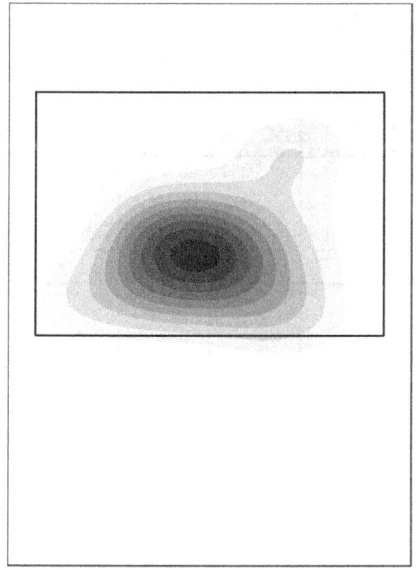

Strike Zone vs RHP

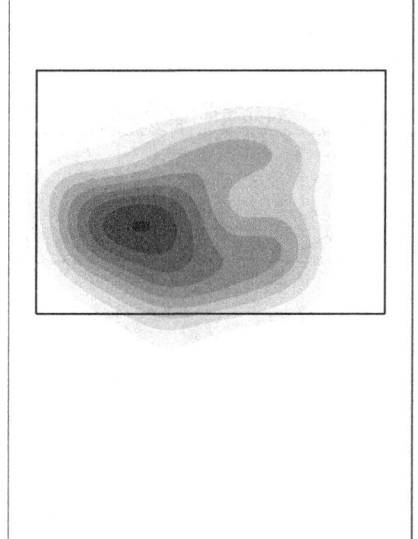

Daniel Descalso UT

Born: 10/19/86 Age: 32 Bats: L Throws: R
Height: 5'10" Weight: 190 Origin: Round 3, 2007 Draft (#112 overall)

YEAR	TEAM	LVL	AGE	PA	R	2B	3B	HR	RBI	BB	K	SB	CS	AVG/OBP/SLG
2016	COL	MLB	29	289	38	12	2	8	38	34	56	3	0	.264/.349/.424
2017	ARI	MLB	30	398	47	16	5	10	51	48	89	4	0	.233/.332/.395
2018	ARI	MLB	31	423	54	22	4	13	57	64	110	0	1	.238/.353/.436
2019	CHN	MLB	32	150	16	7	1	4	17	17	35	1	0	.246/.336/.408

Breakout: 2% Improve: 38% Collapse: 9% Attrition: 7% MLB: 91%
Comparables: Adam Kennedy, Dick McAuliffe, Orlando Hudson

Descalso perennially struggled to provide even league-average offense and his days as a shortstop are all but over. But like a budget wine you decided to age despite the wildly affordable price tag, Descalso has improved over time. He's grown into the Old Player mold and embraced it, letting the strikeouts climb some as he takes more walks and hits for more power. He was a good offensive player in 2018 for the Diamondbacks when they needed one most. With Jake Lamb and Paul Goldschmidt struggling, Descalso carried the team at times early in the season. He did wither a bit down the stretch and his defense isn't what it once was, but he's still a useful piece for a team looking to bolster its bench.

YEAR	TEAM	LVL	AGE	PA	DRC+	VORP	BABIP	BRR	FRAA	WARP
2016	COL	MLB	29	289	94	15.4	.305	3.4	SS(31): -6.0, 1B(16): 0.2	0.5
2017	ARI	MLB	30	398	96	5.8	.283	-3.2	2B(45): 0.9, LF(36): -4.8	0.1
2018	ARI	MLB	31	423	106	22.9	.300	-0.7	2B(52): 3.2, 3B(37): -0.8	1.8
2019	CHN	MLB	32	150	100	5.1	.304	-0.1	SS -1, 3B -1	0.3

Daniel Descalso, continued

Batted Ball Distribution

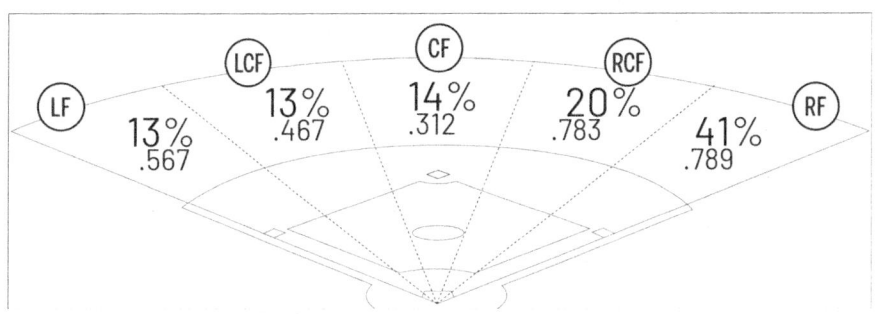

Strike Zone vs LHP   **Strike Zone vs RHP**

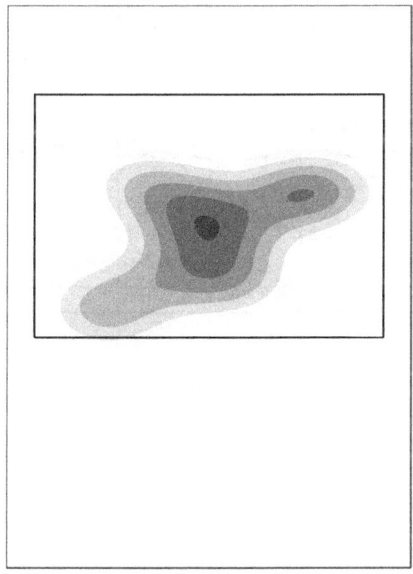 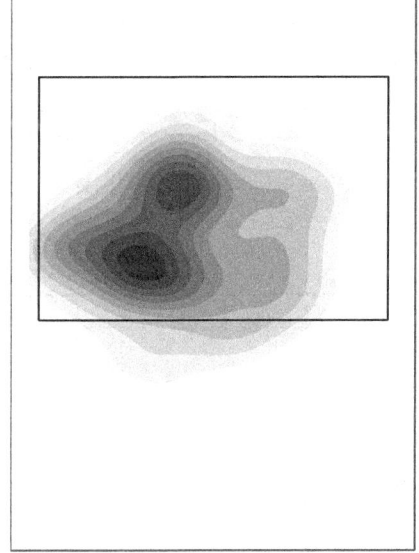

Ian Happ UT

Born: 08/12/94   Age: 24   Bats: B   Throws: R
Height: 6'0"   Weight: 205   Origin: Round 1, 2015 Draft (#9 overall)

YEAR	TEAM	LVL	AGE	PA	R	2B	3B	HR	RBI	BB	K	SB	CS	AVG/OBP/SLG
2016	MYR	A+	21	293	37	16	3	7	42	48	69	10	3	.296/.410/.475
2016	TEN	AA	21	274	35	14	0	8	31	20	60	6	2	.262/.318/.415
2017	IOW	AAA	22	116	21	6	0	9	25	11	27	2	1	.298/.362/.615
2017	CHN	MLB	22	413	62	17	3	24	68	39	129	8	4	.253/.328/.514
2018	CHN	MLB	23	462	56	19	2	15	44	70	167	8	4	.233/.353/.408
2019	CHN	MLB	24	431	56	18	2	16	52	51	145	7	3	.233/.329/.421

Breakout: 7%   Improve: 53%   Collapse: 10%   Attrition: 14%   MLB: 96%
Comparables: Marcell Ozuna, Oswaldo Arcia, Jorge Soler

If Happ is Zobrist 2.0, there have been an awful lot of tweaks to the source code. Happ might walk like Zobrist, but he has struck out more in his first two seasons than Zobrist did in his first five, in almost 900 fewer plate appearances. He can't play the infield like Zobrist either, reflected by his diminished usage there in 2018. It's not like 'upgrading' from XP to Vista, but perhaps we should stop suggesting that Happ can fill the role of one of the most unique players in recent memory and instead recognize him on his own merits.

YEAR	TEAM	LVL	AGE	PA	DRC+	VORP	BABIP	BRR	FRAA	WARP
2016	MYR	A+	21	293	154	26.1	.381	0.2	2B(50): -3.1, LF(6): 0.0	1.2
2016	TEN	AA	21	274	112	9.8	.310	0.4	2B(42): -0.6, RF(7): -1.7	0.4
2017	IOW	AAA	22	116	146	14.0	.319	0.0	2B(16): 1.2, CF(6): 1.0	1.1
2017	CHN	MLB	22	413	106	25.2	.316	3.1	CF(54): 0.7, 2B(44): 0.1	1.5
2018	CHN	MLB	23	462	88	23.0	.362	2.0	CF(63): -7.9, LF(59): -2.5	-0.1
2019	CHN	MLB	24	431	101	17.7	.326	-0.1	CF -5, LF -2	0.8

Ian Happ, continued

Batted Ball Distribution

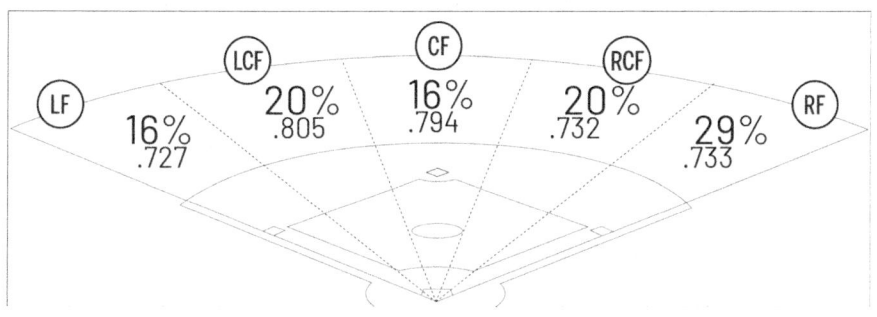

Strike Zone vs LHP

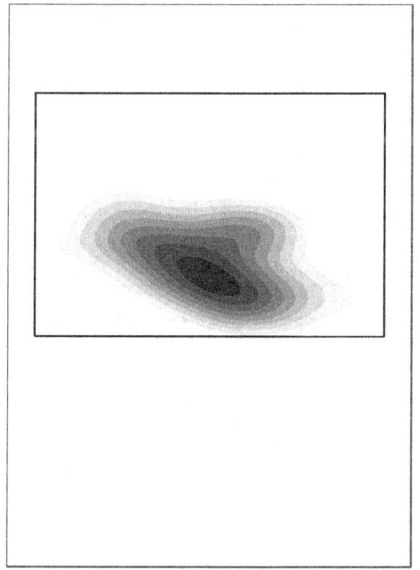

Strike Zone vs RHP

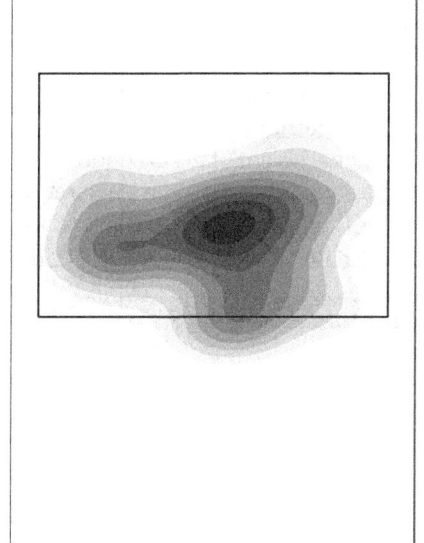

Jason Heyward RF

Born: 08/09/89 Age: 29 Bats: L Throws: L
Height: 6'5" Weight: 240 Origin: Round 1, 2007 Draft (#14 overall)

YEAR	TEAM	LVL	AGE	PA	R	2B	3B	HR	RBI	BB	K	SB	CS	AVG/OBP/SLG
2016	CHN	MLB	26	592	61	27	1	7	49	54	93	11	4	.230/.306/.325
2017	CHN	MLB	27	481	59	15	4	11	59	41	67	4	4	.259/.326/.389
2018	CHN	MLB	28	489	67	23	4	8	57	42	60	1	1	.270/.335/.395
2019	CHN	MLB	29	506	54	21	3	10	49	41	78	6	2	.252/.317/.376

Breakout: 0% Improve: 28% Collapse: 17% Attrition: 18% MLB: 96%
Comparables: Bob Molinaro, Randy Moore, Harvey Kuenn

Heyward's offensive production improved again, albeit ever-so-slightly, and for the first time in a Cubs uniform he was an above-average hitter over the course of the season. The respectable but somewhat dull line is a stark contrast to the dizzying array of changes to both his swing and approach that he made to get here, and the oceans of virtual ink spilled over his efforts to discover an offensive formula that works. Much of the promise from the first half drifted away in the second, as the 28-year-old looked very much like the subpar hitter from his first two years on the North Side. Chicago will take an average Heyward at the plate if he is one of the game's best right fielders, a classification called into doubt by some comparatively pedestrian defensive ratings. The vagaries of fielding metrics allow us to handwave such single-season numbers with the combined weight of his exceptional track record, but it is telling that the first of his opt-out dates passed with barely a thought in November. It's even more telling that the kind of season it would take to imagine Heyward opting out of the final four years of his deal after 2019 feels impossibly far away.

YEAR	TEAM	LVL	AGE	PA	DRC+	VORP	BABIP	BRR	FRAA	WARP
2016	CHN	MLB	26	592	74	-2.6	.266	-0.4	RF(131): -0.2, CF(24): 2.8	-0.3
2017	CHN	MLB	27	481	86	8.6	.284	1.9	RF(120): 10.0, CF(13): 1.0	1.6
2018	CHN	MLB	28	489	94	15.9	.297	3.0	RF(118): 11.5, CF(25): -2.7	2.0
2019	CHN	MLB	29	506	86	8.7	.281	-0.2	RF 4, CF 0	0.9

Jason Heyward, continued

Batted Ball Distribution

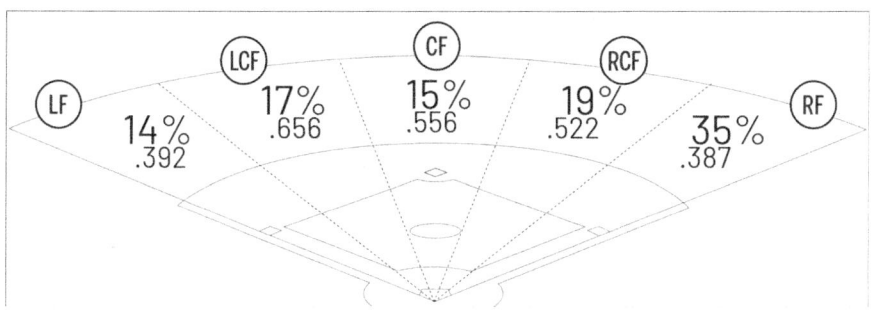

Strike Zone vs LHP

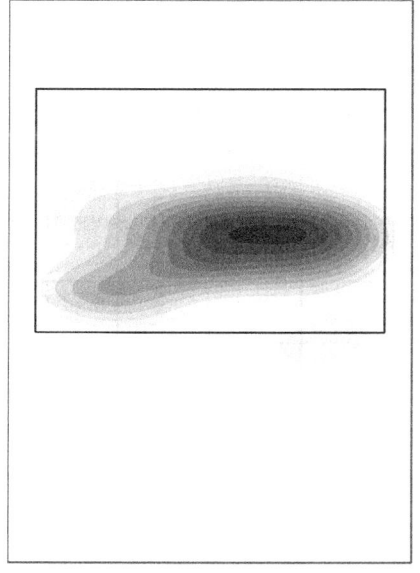

Strike Zone vs RHP

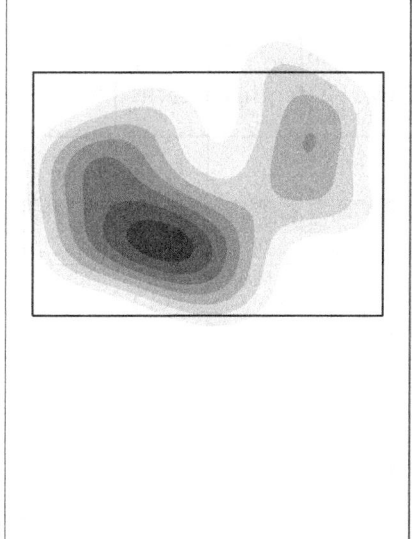

Anthony Rizzo 1B

Born: 08/08/89 Age: 29 Bats: L Throws: L
Height: 6'3" Weight: 240 Origin: Round 6, 2007 Draft (#204 overall)

YEAR	TEAM	LVL	AGE	PA	R	2B	3B	HR	RBI	BB	K	SB	CS	AVG/OBP/SLG
2016	CHN	MLB	26	676	94	43	4	32	109	74	108	3	5	.292/.385/.544
2017	CHN	MLB	27	691	99	32	3	32	109	91	90	10	4	.273/.392/.507
2018	CHN	MLB	28	665	74	29	1	25	101	70	80	6	4	.283/.376/.470
2019	CHN	MLB	29	649	86	33	3	24	88	71	95	7	4	.279/.378/.479

Breakout: 5% Improve: 43% Collapse: 7% Attrition: 2% MLB: 96%
Comparables: Carlos Santana, Todd Helton, Prince Fielder

It can be very disconcerting when even the most dependable players go through prolonged slumps. Even Amazon delivers a package to the wrong address, after all. Rizzo endured his worst month since he was a rookie to start the season, sporting a .149/.259/.189 line at the end of April, partly as the result of a back issue. Normal service soon resumed, as even with another relative slump in June, the first baseman hit a very Rizzo-esque .303/.393/.512 the rest of the way and was one of the few Cubs hitters to not disappear when needed late in the season. In this era of trading contact for power, only a handful of players combine Rizzo's power, patience and ability to avoid strikeouts so effectively. Only 11 hitters have reached 150 home runs over the past five seasons, and Rizzo is the only one to have struck out in fewer than 15 percent of his plate appearances.

YEAR	TEAM	LVL	AGE	PA	DRC+	VORP	BABIP	BRR	FRAA	WARP
2016	CHN	MLB	26	676	139	56.5	.309	-1.2	1B(154): 11.4, 2B(1): -0.2	5.1
2017	CHN	MLB	27	691	126	36.3	.273	-3.2	1B(157): 14.4, 2B(10): -0.3	4.3
2018	CHN	MLB	28	665	128	28.0	.287	-5.8	1B(153): 14.4, P(1): 0.0	4.1
2019	CHN	MLB	29	649	132	36.1	.297	-0.9	1B 9	4.8

Anthony Rizzo, continued

Batted Ball Distribution

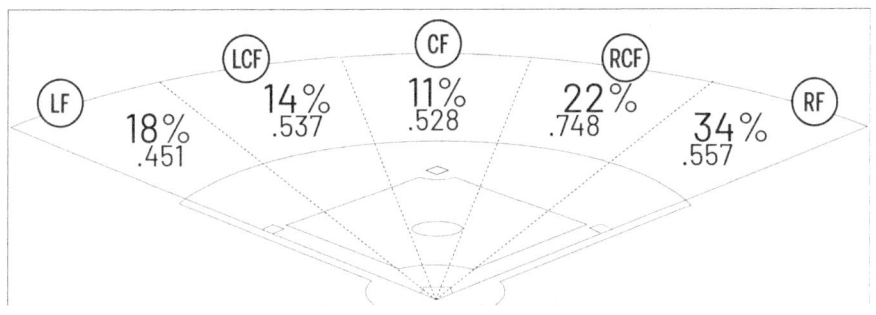

Strike Zone vs LHP

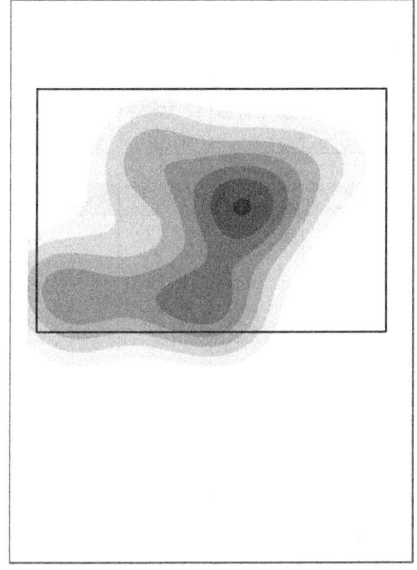

Strike Zone vs RHP

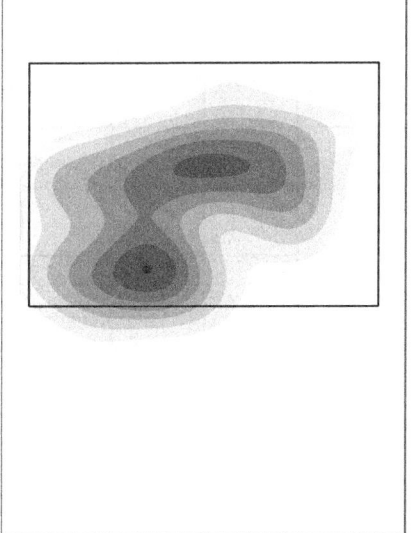

Addison Russell SS

Born: 01/23/94 Age: 25 Bats: R Throws: R
Height: 6'0" Weight: 200 Origin: Round 1, 2012 Draft (#11 overall)

YEAR	TEAM	LVL	AGE	PA	R	2B	3B	HR	RBI	BB	K	SB	CS	AVG/OBP/SLG
2016	CHN	MLB	22	598	67	25	3	21	95	55	135	5	1	.238/.321/.417
2017	CHN	MLB	23	385	52	21	3	12	43	29	91	2	1	.239/.304/.418
2018	CHN	MLB	24	465	52	21	1	5	38	40	99	4	0	.250/.317/.340
2019	CHN	MLB	25	295	32	13	1	7	30	27	66	2	1	.236/.313/.373

Breakout: 6% Improve: 58% Collapse: 7% Attrition: 3% MLB: 96%
Comparables: Khalil Greene, Lyn Lary, Denis Menke

There is so much we could say about Russell, from his failure to live up to expectations on the field to the details of his abusive actions off it—actions which brought his immediate placement on administrative leave and a 40-game suspension. This shouldn't be about Russell, though—it should be about his ex-wife Melisa Reidy and the effects that the abuse had on her. We need to focus on the survivors, listen to them and change the way violence is discussed. We need to recognize that speaking out about domestic violence is incredibly difficult and that the appropriate first response to when a player is accused or suspended is not to dwell on that player, their trade value, contract status or how it might affect their career. Instead it should be to listen to the survivor, talk about the violence and do everything we can to prevent it happening again.

YEAR	TEAM	LVL	AGE	PA	DRC+	VORP	BABIP	BRR	FRAA	WARP
2016	CHN	MLB	22	598	92	33.6	.277	-0.2	SS(148): 3.6	2.4
2017	CHN	MLB	23	385	85	13.7	.289	-0.3	SS(101): 3.4	1.4
2018	CHN	MLB	24	465	81	13.3	.314	-0.8	SS(129): 1.2	1.0
2019	CHN	MLB	25	295	86	6.8	.290	-0.2	SS 3	0.9

Addison Russell, continued

Batted Ball Distribution

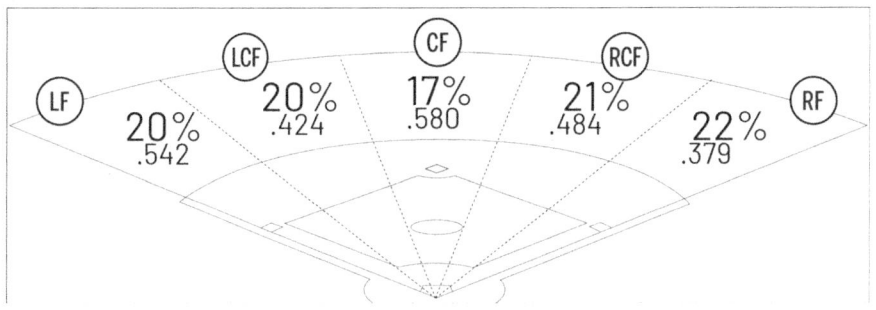

Strike Zone vs LHP

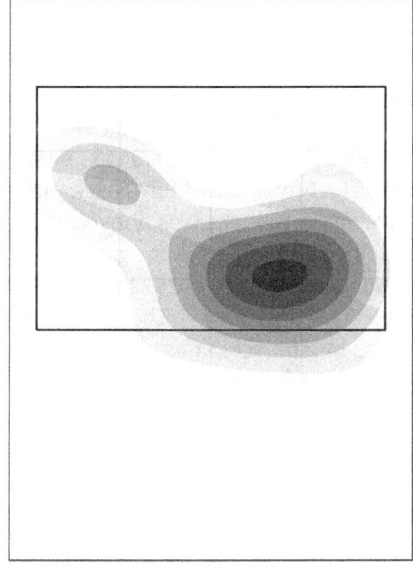

Strike Zone vs RHP

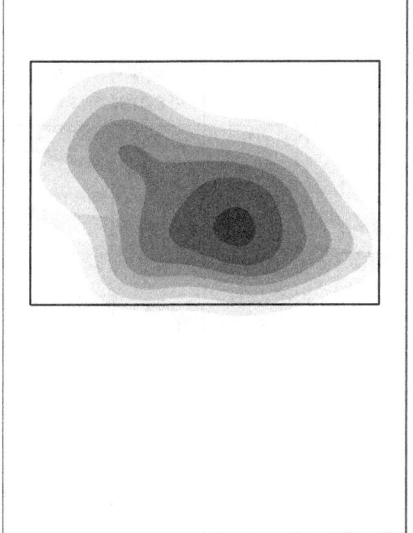

Kyle Schwarber LF

Born: 03/05/93   Age: 26   Bats: L   Throws: R
Height: 6'0"   Weight: 235   Origin: Round 1, 2014 Draft (#4 overall)

YEAR	TEAM	LVL	AGE	PA	R	2B	3B	HR	RBI	BB	K	SB	CS	AVG/OBP/SLG
2016	CHN	MLB	23	5	0	0	0	0	0	1	2	0	0	.000/.200/.000
2017	IOW	AAA	24	44	9	1	0	4	9	8	12	0	0	.343/.477/.714
2017	CHN	MLB	24	486	67	16	1	30	59	59	150	1	1	.211/.315/.467
2018	CHN	MLB	25	510	64	14	3	26	61	78	140	4	3	.238/.356/.467
2019	CHN	MLB	26	504	63	19	2	21	68	59	134	3	2	.240/.333/.436

Breakout: 1%   Improve: 49%   Collapse: 12%   Attrition: 5%   MLB: 98%
Comparables: Ryan Klesko, Mitchell Page, Carlos Gonzalez

Since it became clear that Schwarber was not going to catch in the majors, his fielding prowess has ranked almost equal with pitchers hitting on the list of reasons for the National League to adopt the DH. That all changed in 2018, as profiles which previously used the bat- prefix more than the headline writer at The Daily Gotham now have to account for an entirely competent defensive performance in left field.

To be fair to Schwarber, he did not previously rate as badly in left as the jokes might have led one to believe. Optics are important, and when a slimmed-down, fitter Schwarber emerged in spring looking far less like baseball's favorite Large Adult Son, the chatter about whether this would help his defense began. Some impressive plays with his arm helped, as he finished tied for the league lead in left with 11 assists. While most metrics agreed that he was above-average at the position by season's end, Statcast threw some shade on the improvements, suggesting that Schwarber was one of the game's ten worst outfielders at turning fly balls into outs. That might also suggest that the Cubs have simply used better positioning to address his shortcomings with regards to range, and it does not take away from the fact that his arm has turned into a legitimate weapon.

While poor range at 25 is not an encouraging sign for his long-term future at the position, Schwarber is still relatively inexperienced in the outfield and he doesn't need to be a Gold Glover in left to be a valuable regular on a contender. The primary concern now might be his struggles against southpaws, against whom he has a career .608 OPS. Figuring out how to be as passable against left-handers as he was in left field is the next step in unlocking his full offensive potential.

YEAR	TEAM	LVL	AGE	PA	DRC+	VORP	BABIP	BRR	FRAA	WARP
2016	CHN	MLB	23	5	77	-0.7	.000	0.0	LF(2): 0.0	0.0
2017	IOW	AAA	24	44	168	7.0	.421	-0.1	LF(9): -1.5	0.2
2017	CHN	MLB	24	486	95	14.7	.244	0.6	LF(110): 2.7, C(4): 0.0	1.2
2018	CHN	MLB	25	510	111	21.3	.288	-3.4	LF(120): 2.7	1.9
2019	*CHN*	*MLB*	*26*	*504*	*112*	*21.8*	*.298*	*-0.7*	*LF -2*	*2.0*

Chicago Cubs 2019

Kyle Schwarber, continued

Batted Ball Distribution

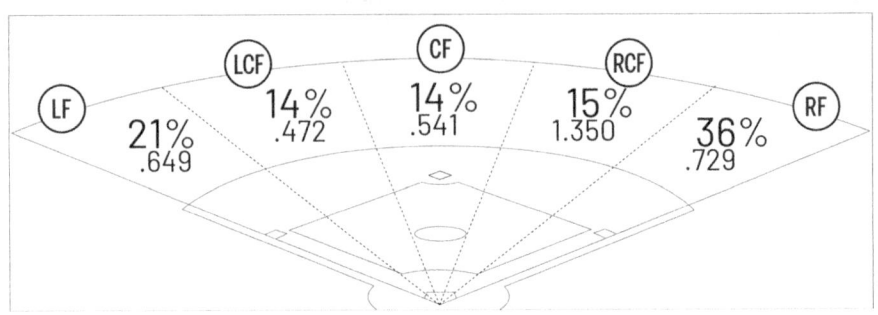

| Strike Zone vs LHP | Strike Zone vs RHP |

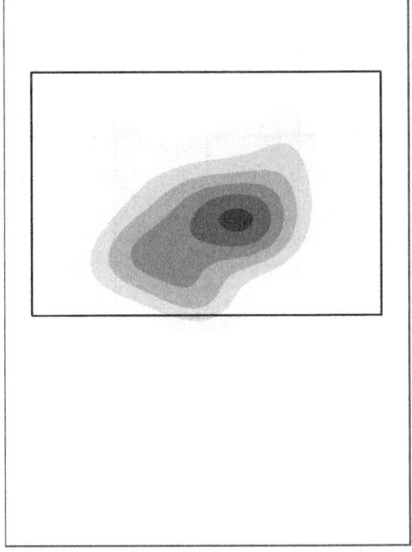

Ben Zobrist 2B

Born: 05/26/81 Age: 38 Bats: B Throws: R
Height: 6'3" Weight: 210 Origin: Round 6, 2004 Draft (#184 overall)

YEAR	TEAM	LVL	AGE	PA	R	2B	3B	HR	RBI	BB	K	SB	CS	AVG/OBP/SLG
2016	CHN	MLB	35	631	94	31	3	18	76	96	82	6	4	.272/.386/.446
2017	CHN	MLB	36	496	58	20	3	12	50	54	71	2	2	.232/.318/.375
2018	CHN	MLB	37	520	67	28	3	9	58	55	60	3	4	.305/.378/.440
2019	CHN	MLB	38	570	68	27	3	11	53	59	86	4	3	.257/.338/.388

Breakout: 0% Improve: 13% Collapse: 21% Attrition: 27% MLB: 77%
Comparables: Brian Giles, Elmer Valo, Enos Slaughter

Zobrist's replacement-level season at the age of 36 had us wondering whether he was set to become the world's most expensive Willie Bloomquist impersonator. Instead he was a bargain version of his near-peak self, putting together his finest year since he was in Tampa Bay, ranking among the league's best in both batting average and on-base percentage while providing his trademark defensive versatility. That versatility is now officially unprecedented: Zobrist is the only player in major league history to play at least 200 games at second, short, and both outfield corners. He is keeping rare company on the offensive side too, as the only qualified hitters in the past decade to get on base more often in their age-37 season are Chipper Jones and David Ortiz.

YEAR	TEAM	LVL	AGE	PA	DRC+	VORP	BABIP	BRR	FRAA	WARP
2016	CHN	MLB	35	631	119	49.2	.290	3.9	2B(119): -7.2, LF(27): -1.6	2.6
2017	CHN	MLB	36	496	87	5.2	.251	-1.3	2B(81): -2.0, LF(36): -0.2	0.1
2018	CHN	MLB	37	520	118	36.0	.331	3.0	2B(63): 4.2, RF(61): 6.1	3.6
2019	CHN	MLB	38	570	98	19.9	.289	-1.2	2B -1, RF 0	1.5

Chicago Cubs 2019

Ben Zobrist, continued

Batted Ball Distribution

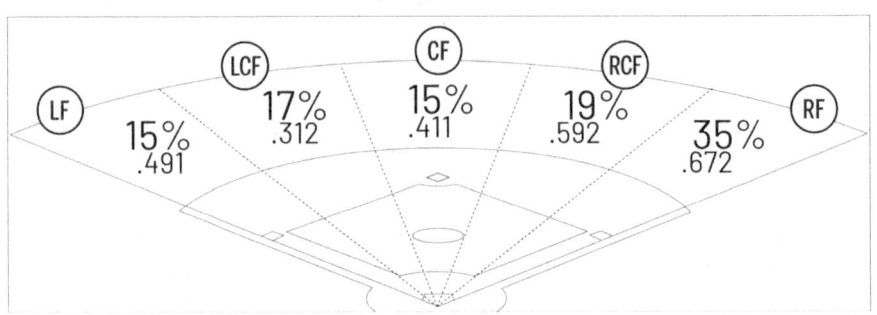

Strike Zone vs LHP

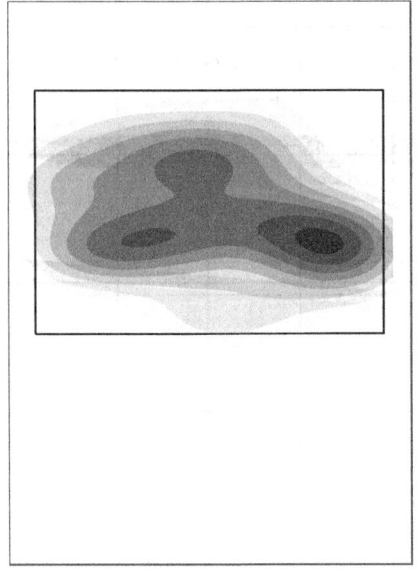

Strike Zone vs RHP

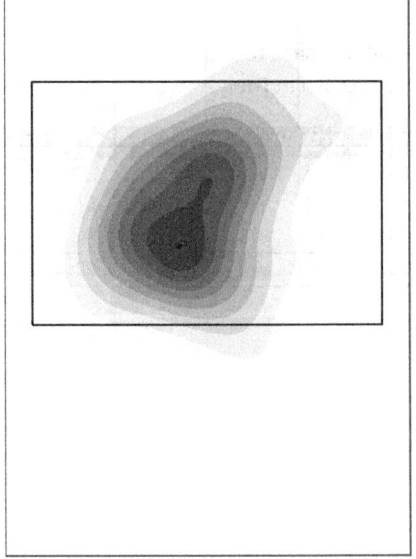

Tony Barnette RHP

Born: 11/09/83 Age: 35 Bats: R Throws: R
Height: 6'1" Weight: 190 Origin: Round 10, 2006 Draft (#297 overall)

YEAR	TEAM	LVL	AGE	W	L	SV	G	GS	IP	H	HR	BB/9	K/9	K	GB%	BABIP
2016	TEX	MLB	32	7	3	0	53	0	60^1	54	4	2.4	7.3	49	48%	.289
2017	TEX	MLB	33	2	1	2	50	0	57^1	64	7	3.5	8.9	57	42%	.348
2018	TEX	MLB	34	2	0	0	22	0	26^1	19	2	1.7	8.9	26	51%	.246
2019	CHN	MLB	35	1	1	0	19	0	20	21	3	3.6	8.2	19	46%	.299

Breakout: 22% Improve: 44% Collapse: 22% Attrition: 16% MLB: 88%
Comparables: Scott Downs, Scott Eyre, Hideki Okajima

On May 23, Barnette allowed two runs to the Yankees in two-thirds of an inning, bumping his season ERA up to 4.15. On July 3, Barnette threw his final pitch of 2018, as he missed the second half with a shoulder injury that just wouldn't go away. Between those two moments, Barnette made 11 appearances, pitching 13 1/3 innings, striking out 12, walking two and allowing 10 hits and just one run. That's an extremely selective sample just to say "0.68 ERA over that period" but … well, he posted an 0.68 ERA over that period. He turned 35 this offseason, but that's not ancient as relievers go, especially for relievers with a sub-1.00 WHIP.

YEAR	TEAM	LVL	AGE	WHIP	ERA	DRA	WARP	MPH	FB%	WHF	CSP
2016	TEX	MLB	32	1.16	2.09	3.92	0.7	94.2	34.4	12.2	43.6
2017	TEX	MLB	33	1.50	5.49	4.28	0.6	94.2	31.7	14.4	43.4
2018	TEX	MLB	34	0.91	2.39	3.93	0.3	94.3	47	12.2	49.9
2019	CHN	MLB	35	1.42	4.62	4.65	0.0	93.0	35.4	13	45.3

Chicago Cubs 2019

Tony Barnette, continued

Pitch Shape vs LHH

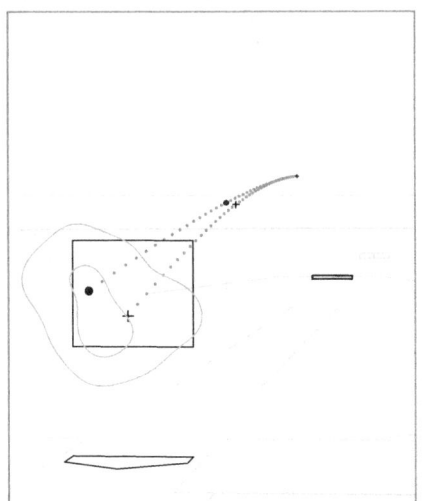

Pitch Shape vs RHH

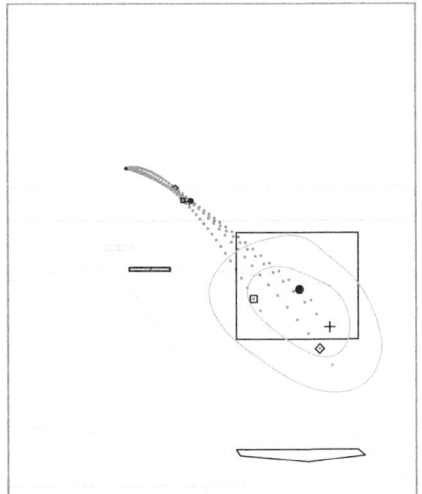

Type	Frequency	Velocity	H Movement	V Movement
● Fastball	28.1%	93.5 [103]	-1.4 [125]	-13 [109]
□ Sinker	18.9%	93.4 [105]	-11.5 [109]	-17.6 [109]
+ Cutter	23.9%	90.4 [109]	5.1 [119]	-20.1 [114]
▲ Changeup	1.2%	87.9 [110]	-9.8 [108]	-27.1 [101]
× Splitter	2.7%	88.3 [114]	-8.4 [99]	-26.4 [113]
▽ Slider	0.7%	87.6 [114]	6.5 [107]	-26.9 [118]
◇ Curveball	24.4%	81.4 [111]	9.8 [108]	-39.4 [120]
⊕ Slow Curveball				
✶ Knuckleball				
▼ Screwball				

Brad Brach   RHP

Born: 04/12/86   Age: 33   Bats: R   Throws: R
Height: 6'6"   Weight: 215   Origin: Round 42, 2008 Draft (#1275 overall)

YEAR	TEAM	LVL	AGE	W	L	SV	G	GS	IP	H	HR	BB/9	K/9	K	GB%	BABIP
2016	BAL	MLB	30	10	4	2	71	0	79	57	7	2.8	10.5	92	43%	.267
2017	BAL	MLB	31	4	5	18	67	0	68	51	7	3.4	9.3	70	42%	.256
2018	BAL	MLB	32	1	2	11	42	0	39	50	4	4.4	8.8	38	48%	.371
2018	ATL	MLB	32	1	2	1	27	0	23^2	22	1	3.4	8.4	22	47%	.296
2019	CHN	MLB	33	2	2	3	44	0	46^1	45	6	3.9	8.5	44	44%	.297

Breakout: 17%   Improve: 42%   Collapse: 30%   Attrition: 10%   MLB: 92%
Comparables: Damaso Marte, Jason Frasor, Fernando Rodney

It's as if Brach suddenly decided Baltimore was bad for his health. Going 47-115 will do that to a person. Brach's season did a 180 in late July when he was traded to the Braves. From there, he went on a string of seven scoreless appearances and allowed just four earned runs in 27 outings. While his strikeout totals remained similar, he received a big boost by cutting his walk rate by an entire walk per nine innings. You might say the move to the NL East would be behind the big change in numbers, but he was solid in important situations against playoff teams like the Red Sox and Brewers. Simply put, Brach was better in Atlanta. A better Brach behooved a better Braves.

YEAR	TEAM	LVL	AGE	WHIP	ERA	DRA	WARP	MPH	FB%	WHF	CSP
2016	BAL	MLB	30	1.04	2.05	2.69	2.1	96.8	60	16	42.6
2017	BAL	MLB	31	1.13	3.18	3.39	1.3	96.4	62.9	12.9	46.6
2018	BAL	MLB	32	1.77	4.85	4.28	0.3	95.3	61.4	14	44.5
2018	ATL	MLB	32	1.31	1.52	3.37	0.4	96.0	52.4	13.7	41.6
2019	CHN	MLB	33	1.41	4.41	4.49	0.2	95.1	59.4	13.9	43.7

Chicago Cubs 2019

Brad Brach, continued

Pitch Shape vs LHH
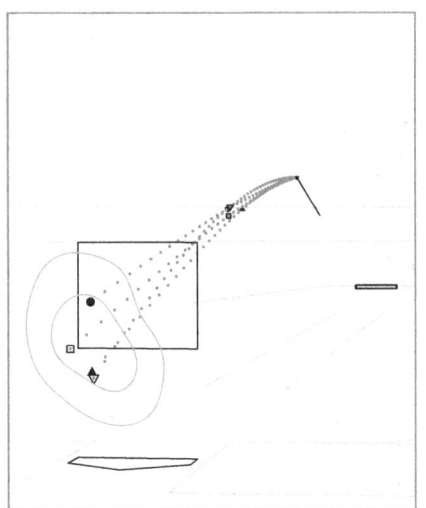

Pitch Shape vs RHH
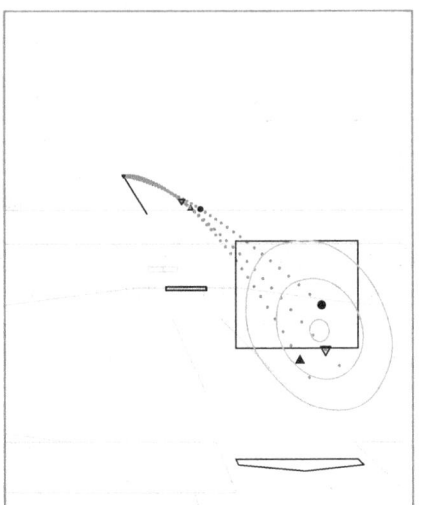

Type	Frequency	Velocity	H Movement	V Movement
● Fastball	53.3%	94.4 [106]	-5.9 [104]	-14.4 [104]
☐ Sinker	4.7%	92.8 [102]	-11.7 [108]	-22.3 [94]
+ Cutter				
▲ Changeup	24.3%	86.4 [104]	-11.5 [99]	-32.5 [85]
✕ Splitter				
▽ Slider	17.7%	84.9 [102]	6.6 [108]	-33.5 [99]
◇ Curveball				
⊕ Slow Curveball				
✳ Knuckleball				
▼ Screwball				

Tyler Chatwood RHP

Born: 12/16/89 Age: 29 Bats: R Throws: R
Height: 6'0" Weight: 185 Origin: Round 2, 2008 Draft (#74 overall)

YEAR	TEAM	LVL	AGE	W	L	SV	G	GS	IP	H	HR	BB/9	K/9	K	GB%	BABIP
2016	COL	MLB	26	12	9	0	27	27	158	147	15	4.0	6.7	117	58%	.286
2017	COL	MLB	27	8	15	1	33	25	147²	136	20	4.7	7.3	120	59%	.283
2018	CHN	MLB	28	4	6	0	24	20	103²	92	9	8.2	7.4	85	55%	.286
2019	CHN	MLB	29	2	3	0	24	5	45	42	4	6.0	7.7	39	54%	.288

Breakout: 15%   Improve: 42%   Collapse: 20%   Attrition: 12%   MLB: 93%
Comparables: Darryl Kile, Whitey Ford, Bob Gibson

Get him out of Coors, they said. He's so much better on the road, they said. Well, Chatwood did give up fewer home runs, and he did have a remarkable season—for all the wrong reasons. Chatwood's control, often lacking, deteriorated to such a point that he led the league in walks despite barely reaching triple digits in innings. It was so bad, in fact, that opposing hitters put up a .403 on-base percentage against Chatwood, a mark that would rank fifth in the majors, better than J.D. Martinez or Christian Yelich. Once Cole Hamels arrived, Chatwood was surplus to requirements, first joining the bullpen—where he walked everyone—then suffering a demotion to Triple-A—where he also walked everyone. We would say that things can presumably only get better from here, but then again, Chatwood seems quite adept at debunking baseball myths.

YEAR	TEAM	LVL	AGE	WHIP	ERA	DRA	WARP	MPH	FB%	WHF	CSP
2016	COL	MLB	26	1.37	3.87	5.43	-0.1	94.8	71.7	8.7	43.3
2017	COL	MLB	27	1.44	4.69	5.28	0.4	96.3	63.7	10.6	43.2
2018	CHN	MLB	28	1.80	5.30	7.28	-2.4	94.9	58.9	8.6	43.4
2019	CHN	MLB	29	1.55	4.99	5.02	0.0	94.7	64.2	9.3	43.3

Chicago Cubs 2019

Tyler Chatwood, continued

Pitch Shape vs LHH

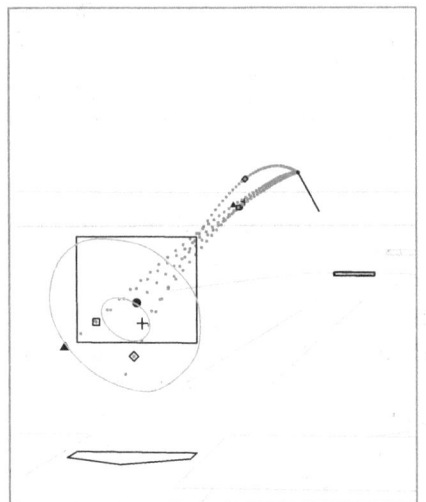

Pitch Shape vs RHH

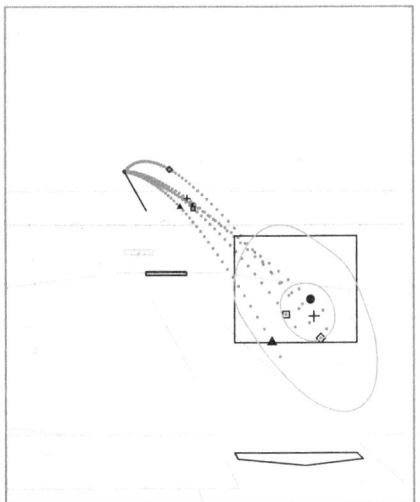

Type	Frequency	Velocity	H Movement	V Movement
● Fastball	33.0%	93.8 [104]	-1.8 [123]	-14 [105]
☐ Sinker	25.9%	93.2 [104]	-11.5 [109]	-17.4 [110]
+ Cutter	25.9%	89.3 [103]	1.7 [99]	-24.5 [97]
▲ Changeup	6.6%	86.8 [106]	-8.9 [113]	-23 [113]
✕ Splitter				
▽ Slider				
◇ Curveball	8.6%	78.6 [100]	8.5 [103]	-53.1 [89]
⊕ Slow Curveball				
✳ Knuckleball				
▼ Screwball				

Steve Cishek RHP

Born: 06/18/86 Age: 33 Bats: R Throws: R
Height: 6'6" Weight: 215 Origin: Round 5, 2007 Draft (#166 overall)

YEAR	TEAM	LVL	AGE	W	L	SV	G	GS	IP	H	HR	BB/9	K/9	K	GB%	BABIP
2016	SEA	MLB	30	4	6	25	62	0	64	44	8	3.0	10.7	76	45%	.242
2017	SEA	MLB	31	1	1	1	23	0	20	13	3	3.2	6.8	15	61%	.185
2017	TBA	MLB	31	2	1	0	26	0	24^2	13	0	2.6	9.5	26	52%	.220
2018	CHN	MLB	32	4	3	4	80	0	70^1	45	5	3.6	10.0	78	49%	.238
2019	CHN	MLB	33	2	2	3	44	0	46^1	41	5	3.9	9.5	49	47%	.291

Breakout: 17% Improve: 41% Collapse: 33% Attrition: 10% MLB: 93%
Comparables: Damaso Marte, Fernando Rodney, Tyler Clippard

Craig Kimbrel. Aroldis Chapman. Kenley Jansen. Dellin Betances. Clayton Kershaw. If one of the first names springing to mind in response is Cishek's, you probably have an unhealthy obsession with the veteran sidearmer, or simply spend a lot of time looking at leaderboards. Those players are the active career ERA leaders, among whom Cishek ranks eighth. Neither the peripherals nor the eye test suggest that he is in that class, and yet his delivery and arsenal clearly enable him to consistently induce poor contact, as his .232 BABIP over the past three seasons can attest. The command can waver and free passes can be a problem against left-handers, the constant nemesis of those with an arm slot as low as Cishek's. For righties, he genuinely is one of the most challenging pitchers to face in all of baseball, making that stellar company far less ridiculous than it seems.

YEAR	TEAM	LVL	AGE	WHIP	ERA	DRA	WARP	MPH	FB%	WHF	CSP
2016	SEA	MLB	30	1.02	2.81	3.08	1.4	93.9	48.7	11.9	44.5
2017	SEA	MLB	31	1.00	3.15	4.78	0.1	92.1	51.5	8.2	46.5
2017	TBA	MLB	31	0.81	1.09	3.41	0.5	92.4	49.5	13.7	44.3
2018	CHN	MLB	32	1.04	2.18	4.68	0.2	92.3	61.6	12	46.7
2019	CHN	MLB	33	1.31	3.97	4.14	0.4	91.7	54.7	11.6	45.2

Steve Cishek, continued

Pitch Shape vs LHH

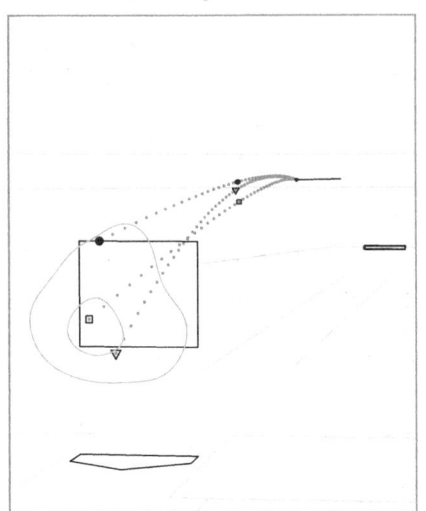

Pitch Shape vs RHH

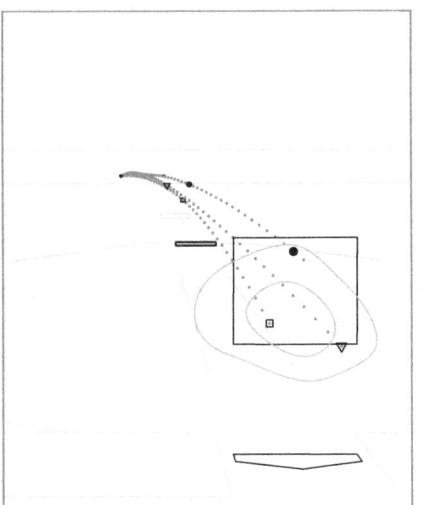

Type	Frequency	Velocity	H Movement	V Movement
● Fastball	15.7%	90.9 [95]	-9.1 [89]	-20.4 [85]
□ Sinker	45.9%	90.9 [92]	-14.5 [84]	-26.5 [80]
+ Cutter	0.7%	91.1 [114]	-3.9 [66]	-21.3 [110]
▲ Changeup	0.2%	84.7 [97]	-14 [86]	-31.7 [87]
✕ Splitter	0.1%	83.9 [90]	-13.2 [80]	-31.7 [91]
▽ Slider	37.4%	78.1 [71]	14.1 [140]	-41.3 [75]
◇ Curveball				
⊕ Slow Curveball				
✶ Knuckleball				
▼ Screwball				

Yu Darvish RHP

Born: 08/16/86   Age: 32   Bats: R   Throws: R
Height: 6'5"   Weight: 220   Origin: International Free Agent, 2012

YEAR	TEAM	LVL	AGE	W	L	SV	G	GS	IP	H	HR	BB/9	K/9	K	GB%	BABIP
2016	FRI	AA	29	1	1	0	5	5	20	14	1	3.2	10.8	24	50%	.277
2016	TEX	MLB	29	7	5	0	17	17	100[1]	81	12	2.8	11.8	132	40%	.290
2017	TEX	MLB	30	6	9	0	22	22	137	115	20	3.0	9.7	148	42%	.275
2017	LAN	MLB	30	4	3	0	9	9	49[2]	44	7	2.4	11.1	61	45%	.308
2018	CHN	MLB	31	1	3	0	8	8	40	36	7	4.7	11.0	49	42%	.293
2019	CHN	MLB	32	9	8	0	29	24	141	125	16	3.4	9.8	155	42%	.293

Breakout: 16%   Improve: 51%   Collapse: 17%   Attrition: 2%   MLB: 95%
Comparables: Ron Guidry, Jorge De La Rosa, Jakie May

Of all the universes in which Darvish signed a six-year, $126 million deal, 2018 was surely the version of his first year plucked directly from the Darkest Timeline. His season wasn't quite over in the time it takes to go and collect some pizza, but Theo Epstein left the offseason with an apparently strengthened rotation and suddenly found that his acquisitions had turned into the pitching equivalent of a burning apartment. Darvish made just three good starts, struggled through several more before landing on the DL with triceps tightness, and was ultimately ruled out for the season after months of uncertainty. The final definitive diagnosis of Darvish's elbow woes, a stress reaction, also doubled as a comment on the likely response of Epstein and most Cubs fans every time another piece of news broke. At least the 32-year-old should be ready for Spring Training, in time for another roll of the dice.

YEAR	TEAM	LVL	AGE	WHIP	ERA	DRA	WARP	MPH	FB%	WHF	CSP
2016	FRI	AA	29	1.05	2.25	2.99	0.5				
2016	TEX	MLB	29	1.12	3.41	2.97	2.7	97.1	69	14	48.6
2017	TEX	MLB	30	1.17	4.01	3.95	2.5	96.5	66.6	12.7	49.3
2017	LAN	MLB	30	1.15	3.44	2.47	1.7	96.4	66.6	14	46.6
2018	CHN	MLB	31	1.42	4.95	4.73	0.3	96.1	69.1	11.3	50.4
2019	CHN	MLB	32	1.26	3.82	3.96	1.8	95.6	67	12.9	48.9

Chicago Cubs 2019

Yu Darvish, continued

Pitch Shape vs LHH

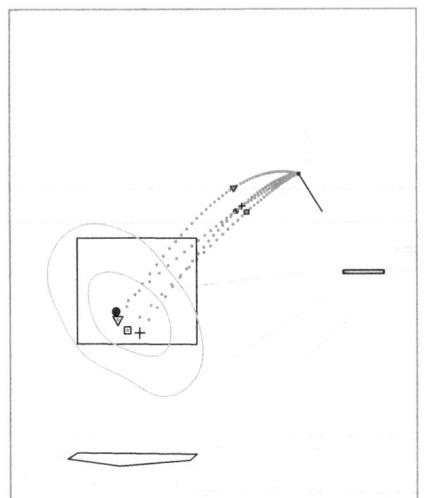

Pitch Shape vs RHH

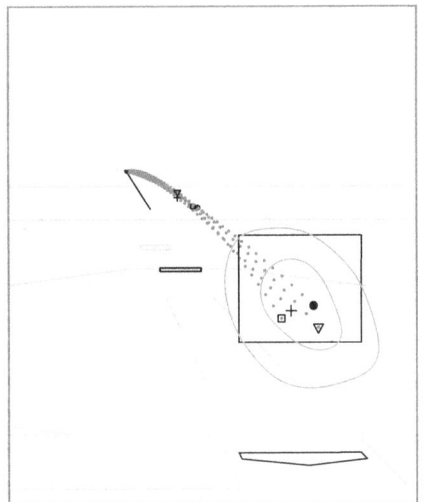

Type	Frequency	Velocity	H Movement	V Movement
● Fastball	37.8%	94.8 [107]	-4.1 [112]	-12.8 [109]
□ Sinker	17.8%	94.2 [109]	-11.6 [108]	-19.7 [102]
+ Cutter	13.4%	89.9 [107]	4.2 [113]	-22.5 [105]
▲ Changeup	2.3%	90.1 [119]	-6.6 [125]	-23 [113]
× Splitter	1.9%	90.6 [127]	-5.6 [110]	-26.5 [113]
▽ Slider	23.5%	85 [103]	11.2 [127]	-32.5 [101]
◇ Curveball	3.1%	76 [91]	11.6 [116]	-54.4 [86]
⊕ Slow Curveball	0.1%	64.8 [94]	10.5 [100]	-71.9 [94]
✳ Knuckleball				
▼ Screwball				

Brian Duensing LHP
Born: 02/22/83 Age: 36 Bats: L Throws: L
Height: 6'0" Weight: 200 Origin: Round 3, 2005 Draft (#84 overall)

YEAR	TEAM	LVL	AGE	W	L	SV	G	GS	IP	H	HR	BB/9	K/9	K	GB%	BABIP
2016	OMA	AAA	33	1	0	2	12	0	20^1	16	0	2.2	8.4	19	50%	.276
2016	BAL	MLB	33	1	0	0	14	0	13^1	13	2	2.0	6.8	10	26%	.275
2017	CHN	MLB	34	1	1	0	68	0	62^1	58	6	2.6	8.8	61	49%	.306
2018	CHN	MLB	35	3	0	1	48	0	37^2	42	6	6.9	5.7	24	43%	.298
2019	CHN	MLB	36	1	1	0	24	0	25^2	28	4	4.7	6.8	20	44%	.296

Breakout: 24% Improve: 37% Collapse: 22% Attrition: 5% MLB: 65%
Comparables: Matt Lindstrom, Bob Locker, Steve Kline

As if we needed any more evidence to indicate that relievers are volatile, Duensing went directly from his best ever relief season to his worst. The increased changeup usage that helped him to neutralize righties persisted, while the results did not. It sounds like hyperbole to say that opposite-handed hitters got on base like Mike Trout against Duensing, when in reality that is insufficient: their OBP was ten points *higher* than Trout's in 2018. The right-handers have always been the bigger problem, yet the peripherals were far from impressive against lefties either. Although his numbers might suggest he simply lost the plate, Duensing threw more pitches in the zone than he did in 2017. Hitters simply went after those more, and weren't buying what he was selling when he tried to get them to chase. Whether the cause was the left shoulder inflammation that ultimately landed him on the DL in August or not, Duensing needs to demonstrate that volatility works both ways if he is to remain in the majors much longer.

YEAR	TEAM	LVL	AGE	WHIP	ERA	DRA	WARP	MPH	FB%	WHF	CSP
2016	OMA	AAA	33	1.03	3.10	3.47	0.3				
2016	BAL	MLB	33	1.20	4.05	6.32	-0.2	94.4	55.1	9.8	50.9
2017	CHN	MLB	34	1.22	2.74	4.04	0.8	93.6	48.9	11.3	42.2
2018	CHN	MLB	35	1.88	7.65	7.34	-1.0	92.9	54.6	9.5	46.9
2019	CHN	MLB	36	1.60	5.85	5.65	-0.3	92.1	50.7	10.2	45.3

Chicago Cubs 2019

Brian Duensing, continued

Pitch Shape vs LHH
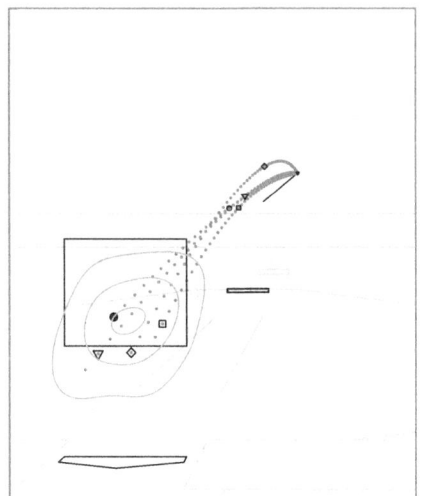

Pitch Shape vs RHH
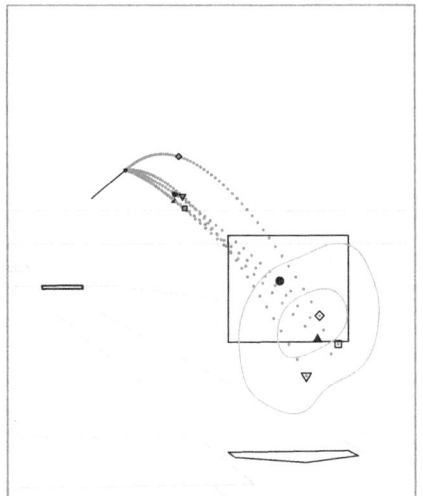

Type	Frequency	Velocity	H Movement	V Movement
● Fastball	32.2%	91.8 [98]	4.3 [111]	-16.4 [98]
□ Sinker	22.4%	90.9 [92]	13 [97]	-21.2 [97]
+ Cutter				
▲ Changeup	14.6%	85.6 [101]	13.6 [88]	-25.9 [104]
× Splitter				
▽ Slider	18.4%	81.2 [85]	-7.9 [113]	-35.4 [93]
◇ Curveball	12.4%	72 [76]	-8.5 [103]	-59.4 [74]
⊕ Slow Curveball				
✳ Knuckleball				
▼ Screwball				

Carl Edwards Jr. RHP

Born: 09/03/91 Age: 27 Bats: R Throws: R
Height: 6'3" Weight: 170 Origin: Round 48, 2011 Draft (#1464 overall)

YEAR	TEAM	LVL	AGE	W	L	SV	G	GS	IP	H	HR	BB/9	K/9	K	GB%	BABIP
2016	IOW	AAA	24	1	1	1	24	0	25^1	17	1	6.0	12.4	35	40%	.286
2016	CHN	MLB	24	0	1	2	36	0	36	15	4	3.5	13.0	52	51%	.162
2017	CHN	MLB	25	5	4	0	73	0	66^1	29	6	5.2	12.8	94	46%	.193
2018	CHN	MLB	26	3	2	0	58	0	52	36	2	5.5	11.6	67	32%	.281
2019	CHN	MLB	27	2	3	5	49	0	51	40	6	5.1	11.2	64	40%	.280

Breakout: 30% Improve: 50% Collapse: 36% Attrition: 12% MLB: 95%
Comparables: Daniel Bard, Carlos Marmol, Bobby Jenks

The unprecedented levels of BABIP suppression that Edwards enjoyed through the first hundred-plus innings of his career finally normalized, yet hardly to his detriment. That good fortune instead manifested in a miniscule home run rate, which helped the slight right-hander to a career-best ERA. Somehow, this came about despite a fundamental change in the batted ball mix, as Edwards lost his ability to generate grounders and experienced a huge jump in both fly-ball and line-drive rate. With his premium velocity and the huge horizontal movement on his offerings, he should remain difficult to hit, borne out by that BABIP and the career ISO allowed of under .100. This tightrope act gets ever more precarious as the strikeout rate drops, though, and Edwards shows no signs of curtailing the walks.

YEAR	TEAM	LVL	AGE	WHIP	ERA	DRA	WARP	MPH	FB%	WHF	CSP
2016	IOW	AAA	24	1.34	4.26	2.24	0.8				
2016	CHN	MLB	24	0.81	3.75	2.34	1.1	97.6	73.2	18.6	41.4
2017	CHN	MLB	25	1.01	2.98	3.05	1.6	96.8	70	16.1	42.8
2018	CHN	MLB	26	1.31	2.60	4.39	0.3	96.2	75.8	15.6	42.6
2019	CHN	MLB	27	1.32	4.05	4.21	0.4	96.2	73.9	16.5	42.9

Carl Edwards Jr., continued

Pitch Shape vs LHH

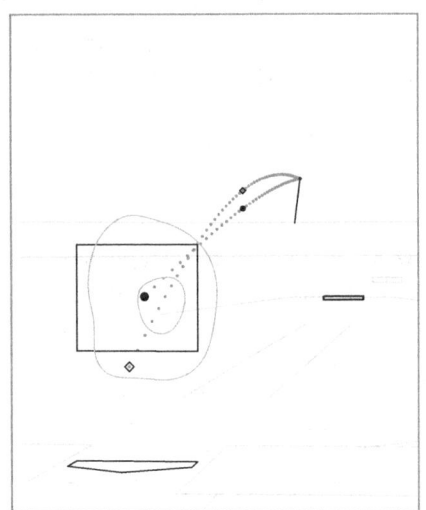

Pitch Shape vs RHH

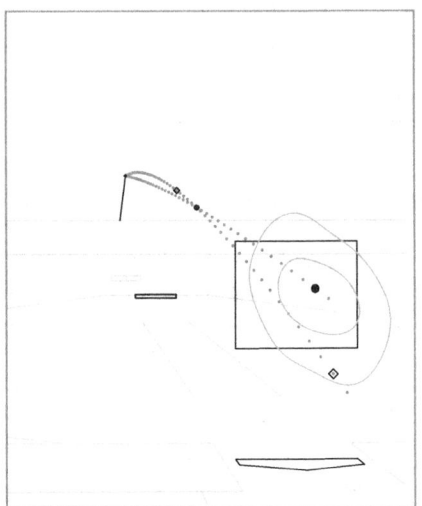

Type	Frequency	Velocity	H Movement	V Movement
● Fastball	75.8%	95 [108]	2 [140]	-12.8 [109]
☐ Sinker				
+ Cutter				
▲ Changeup	0.2%	91.7 [125]	-6.8 [124]	-18.2 [127]
✕ Splitter				
▽ Slider				
◇ Curveball	24.0%	80.7 [108]	10.1 [110]	-48 [100]
⊕ Slow Curveball				
✳ Knuckleball				
▼ Screwball				

Kendall Graveman RHP

Born: 12/21/90 Age: 28 Bats: R Throws: R
Height: 6'2" Weight: 200 Origin: Round 8, 2013 Draft (#235 overall)

YEAR	TEAM	LVL	AGE	W	L	SV	G	GS	IP	H	HR	BB/9	K/9	K	GB%	BABIP
2016	OAK	MLB	25	10	11	0	31	31	186	196	22	2.3	5.2	108	53%	.290
2017	NAS	AAA	26	0	1	0	3	3	10	18	1	3.6	6.3	7	46%	.425
2017	OAK	MLB	26	6	4	0	19	19	105¹	114	12	2.7	6.0	70	52%	.313
2018	OAK	MLB	27	1	5	0	7	7	34¹	44	9	3.4	7.1	27	57%	.324
2018	NAS	AAA	27	2	1	0	4	4	24	35	3	2.6	6.0	16	56%	.405
2019	CHN	MLB	28	4	4	0	11	11	64¹	64	7	3.0	7.0	50	51%	.308

Breakout: 8% Improve: 47% Collapse: 18% Attrition: 23% MLB: 89%
Comparables: Shawn Hill, Nick Blackburn, Sergio Mitre

The list of good things that happened to Graveman in 2018 basically went "started on Opening Day." The list of bad things included two demotions to Triple-A, the unsightly performance you can see above, Tommy John surgery and being non-tendered. He's unlikely to pitch in 2019 given the timing of the surgery. Nothing we've seen so far indicates he'll be anything more than a fourth starter in 2020 even though he's out there throwing a heavy, mid-90s sinker. Maybe he'll add some kind of wrinkle, like taking his secondaries to a whole new level, in his time off; maybe, similarly, this cat will stop eating plastic bags.

YEAR	TEAM	LVL	AGE	WHIP	ERA	DRA	WARP	MPH	FB%	WHF	CSP
2016	OAK	MLB	25	1.31	4.11	4.94	0.9	95.3	61.8	8.1	48.6
2017	NAS	AAA	26	2.20	7.20	4.47	0.1				
2017	OAK	MLB	26	1.39	4.19	5.42	0.2	95.4	68.9	7.4	43.4
2018	OAK	MLB	27	1.66	7.60	5.38	0.0	95.5	57.2	8	44.4
2018	NAS	AAA	27	1.75	4.50	4.56	0.3				
2019	CHN	MLB	28	1.33	4.19	4.63	0.5	94.8	64	7.9	45.4

Kendall Graveman, continued

Pitch Shape vs LHH

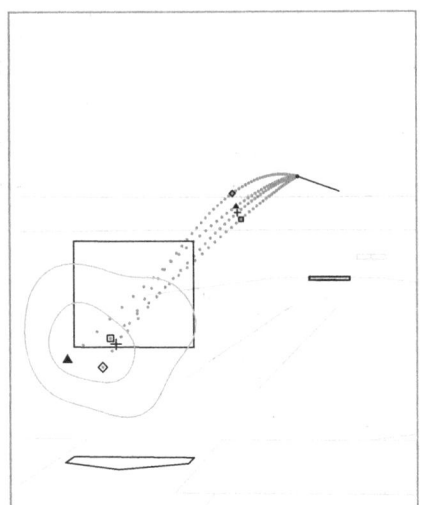

Pitch Shape vs RHH

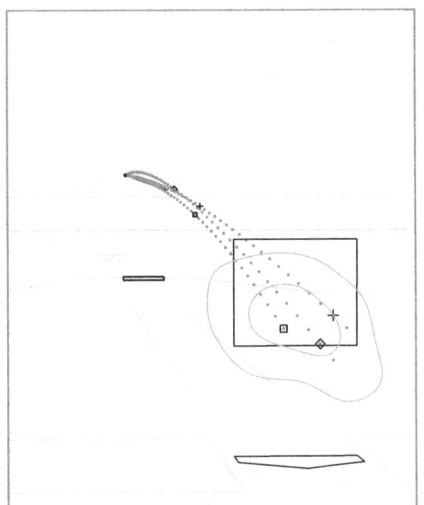

Type	Frequency	Velocity	H Movement	V Movement
● Fastball	3.2%	94.8 [107]	-9 [89]	-13.2 [108]
□ Sinker	54.0%	94.3 [109]	-14.6 [83]	-17.5 [109]
+ Cutter	14.9%	91 [113]	-1.6 [80]	-20.6 [112]
▲ Changeup	15.0%	87 [107]	-12.5 [94]	-29 [95]
× Splitter				
▽ Slider				
◇ Curveball	12.9%	81.7 [112]	9.8 [108]	-41.3 [115]
⊕ Slow Curveball				
✱ Knuckleball				
▼ Screwball				

Cole Hamels LHP

Born: 12/27/83 Age: 35 Bats: L Throws: L
Height: 6'4" Weight: 205 Origin: Round 1, 2002 Draft (#17 overall)

YEAR	TEAM	LVL	AGE	W	L	SV	G	GS	IP	H	HR	BB/9	K/9	K	GB%	BABIP
2016	TEX	MLB	32	15	5	0	32	32	200^2	185	24	3.5	9.0	200	50%	.299
2017	TEX	MLB	33	11	6	0	24	24	148	125	18	3.2	6.4	105	48%	.251
2018	TEX	MLB	34	5	9	0	20	20	114^1	115	23	3.3	9.0	114	45%	.296
2018	CHN	MLB	34	4	3	0	12	12	76^1	61	6	2.7	8.7	74	49%	.286
2019	CHN	MLB	35	11	11	0	30	30	180	166	21	3.2	8.4	168	46%	.290

Breakout: 19% Improve: 38% Collapse: 30% Attrition: 12% MLB: 88%
Comparables: J.A. Happ, Justin Verlander, Jorge De La Rosa

Every now and again, decline phases seem to go almost exactly as we expect. The warning signs around Hamels had been flashing for a little while, so when the 34-year-old labored through four months with Texas it appeared that this was simply one of those cases. His chances of landing on a contender seemed to have been spectacularly torpedoed by a July in which he allowed 21 runs in just 17 innings. The Cubs were undeterred, though, and brought Hamels to Wrigley at the deadline, where he promptly looked like an ace again. It may have seemed as though Chicago fixed Hamels, when in truth the major changes—mechanical improvements that brought a velocity bump, and increased four-seam usage instead of the sinker—were both in progress well before he arrived in Illinois. He'll return in 2019 with the aim of staying ahead of the aging curve.

YEAR	TEAM	LVL	AGE	WHIP	ERA	DRA	WARP	MPH	FB%	WHF	CSP
2016	TEX	MLB	32	1.31	3.32	3.91	3.3	94.9	66.7	13.1	42.3
2017	TEX	MLB	33	1.20	4.20	5.41	0.3	93.5	66.4	10	45.7
2018	TEX	MLB	34	1.37	4.72	5.17	0.2	93.3	60.4	13	45.7
2018	CHN	MLB	34	1.10	2.36	3.46	1.6	94.5	60.4	12.6	46.3
2019	CHN	MLB	35	1.27	4.10	4.24	1.7	92.8	62.7	11.9	44.1

Chicago Cubs 2019

Cole Hamels, continued

Pitch Shape vs LHH	Pitch Shape vs RHH
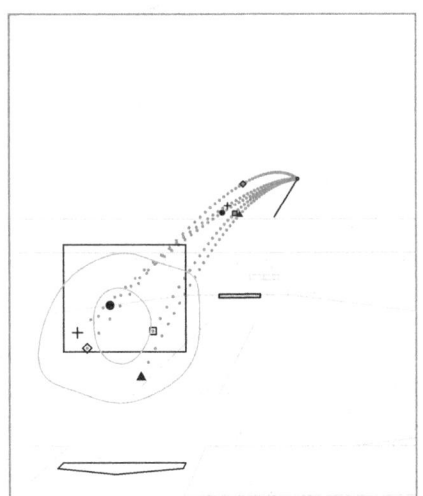	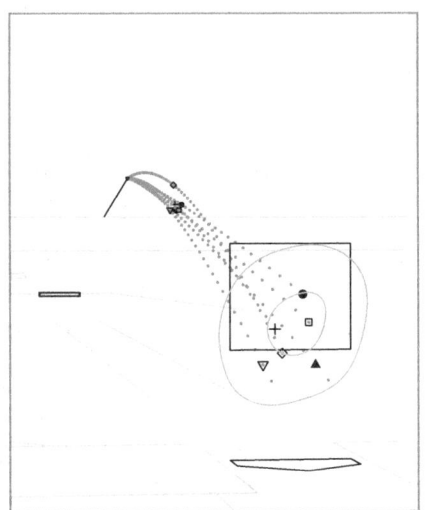

Type	Frequency	Velocity	H Movement	V Movement
● Fastball	30.2%	92.8 [101]	7 [98]	-14.6 [104]
□ Sinker	15.0%	91.9 [97]	13.7 [91]	-20.5 [99]
+ Cutter	18.0%	88 [96]	-0.6 [93]	-24.5 [97]
▲ Changeup	18.8%	83.9 [94]	12.3 [95]	-26.8 [101]
× Splitter				
▽ Slider	4.8%	85.4 [104]	-0.2 [80]	-31.1 [106]
◇ Curveball	13.1%	79.2 [103]	-4.3 [85]	-48 [100]
⊕ Slow Curveball				
✳ Knuckleball				
▼ Screwball				

Kyle Hendricks   RHP

Born: 12/07/89   Age: 29   Bats: R   Throws: R
Height: 6'3"   Weight: 190   Origin: Round 8, 2011 Draft (#264 overall)

YEAR	TEAM	LVL	AGE	W	L	SV	G	GS	IP	H	HR	BB/9	K/9	K	GB%	BABIP
2016	CHN	MLB	26	16	8	0	31	30	190	142	15	2.1	8.1	170	50%	.250
2017	CHN	MLB	27	7	5	0	24	24	139^2	126	17	2.6	7.9	123	52%	.281
2018	CHN	MLB	28	14	11	0	33	33	199	184	22	2.0	7.3	161	49%	.281
2019	*CHN*	*MLB*	*29*	*10*	*10*	*0*	*29*	*29*	*165^1*	*154*	*19*	*2.6*	*7.9*	*145*	*48%*	*.287*

Breakout: 16%   `Improve: 45%   Collapse: 18%   Attrition: 10%   MLB: 96%
Comparables: Garrett Richards, Dallas Keuchel, Johnny Cueto

Only four active pitchers have started more than 100 games and still have a career ERA lower than Hendricks: Clayton Kershaw, Jacob deGrom, Chris Sale and Madison Bumgarner. Hendricks could not quite keep his career mark below 3.00, but the caliber of the company is a testament to the Professor's exceptional command and sequencing. It's even more impressive when you consider that the only two pitchers with lower average four-seam velocity were Brent Suter and Jason Vargas. There's always a temptation to point out how quickly things can go wrong for a player with an 88-mph fastball if everything is not exactly right, but Hendricks has spent most of his 789 major league innings getting everything exactly right.

YEAR	TEAM	LVL	AGE	WHIP	ERA	DRA	WARP	MPH	FB%	WHF	CSP
2016	CHN	MLB	26	0.98	2.13	2.62	6.0	90.2	65.1	10.5	45.3
2017	CHN	MLB	27	1.19	3.03	3.45	3.3	87.6	64.1	9	46.7
2018	CHN	MLB	28	1.15	3.44	3.13	5.0	88.5	61.8	9.7	50.4
2019	*CHN*	*MLB*	*29*	*1.20*	*3.97*	*4.09*	*1.8*	*88.1*	*63.3*	*9.7*	*47.9*

Chicago Cubs 2019

Kyle Hendricks, continued

Pitch Shape vs LHH

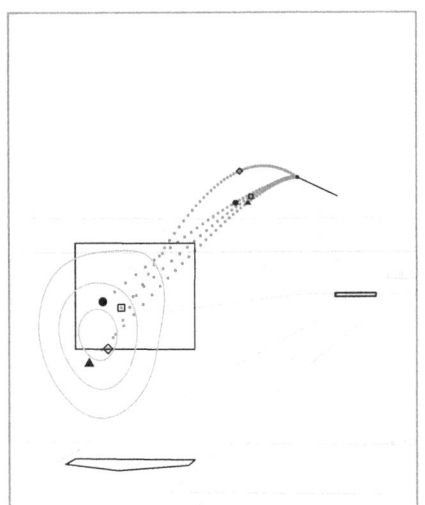

Pitch Shape vs RHH

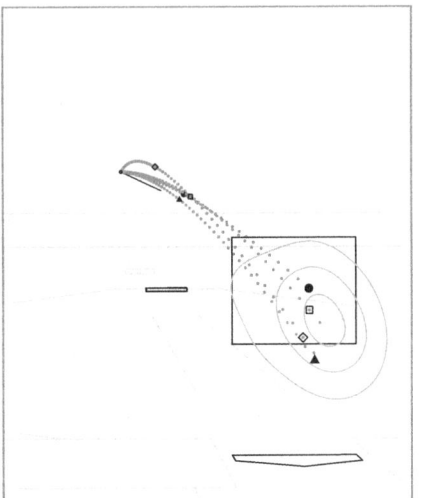

Type	Frequency	Velocity	H Movement	V Movement
● Fastball	17.5%	87.7 [84]	-3 [117]	-16.9 [96]
☐ Sinker	44.3%	87.1 [73]	-10.1 [121]	-23 [91]
+ Cutter				
▲ Changeup	30.7%	79 [75]	-9 [112]	-28.8 [96]
✕ Splitter				
▽ Slider				
◇ Curveball	7.5%	72.2 [77]	13.8 [125]	-58 [78]
⊕ Slow Curveball				
✳ Knuckleball				
▼ Screwball				

Brandon Kintzler RHP

Born: 08/01/84 Age: 34 Bats: R Throws: R
Height: 6'0" Weight: 194 Origin: Round 40, 2004 Draft (#1182 overall)

YEAR	TEAM	LVL	AGE	W	L	SV	G	GS	IP	H	HR	BB/9	K/9	K	GB%	BABIP
2016	ROC	AAA	31	4	1	0	10	0	15^1	15	0	1.8	6.5	11	56%	.326
2016	MIN	MLB	31	0	2	17	54	0	54^1	59	5	1.3	5.8	35	63%	.310
2017	MIN	MLB	32	2	2	28	45	0	45^1	41	3	2.2	5.4	27	54%	.273
2017	WAS	MLB	32	2	1	1	27	0	26	25	2	1.7	4.2	12	57%	.267
2018	WAS	MLB	33	1	2	2	45	0	42^2	40	2	2.7	6.5	31	49%	.302
2018	CHN	MLB	33	2	1	0	25	0	18	27	3	4.5	6.0	12	53%	.381
2019	CHN	MLB	34	1	1	0	24	0	25^2	28	3	3.5	6.2	18	52%	.301

Breakout: 20% Improve: 33% Collapse: 25% Attrition: 8% MLB: 77%
Comparables: Brian Duensing, Paul Quantrill, Matt Albers

Eyebrows were raised when the Nationals shipped Kintzler to Chicago for Jhon Romero, an unheralded reliever at High-A. The salacious rumors for the swap soon followed, with whispers that the real reason for the deal was that in a clubhouse leakier than the Oakland Coliseum's plumbing, Washington believed Kintzler was the prime source responsible for a Jeff Passan story on team unrest. By the time the season was over, one had to wonder whether the Nationals simply had perfect timing. Kintzler's spell in Chicago was a study in how one can pitch to contact with below-average command. To make matters worse, his ground-ball rate has dropped from elite to simply above-average. On his current trajectory (his DRA has now increased for the fourth straight season) it won't be leaks to the press that keep him out of a major-league clubhouse for good.

YEAR	TEAM	LVL	AGE	WHIP	ERA	DRA	WARP	MPH	FB%	WHF	CSP
2016	ROC	AAA	31	1.17	3.52	3.20	0.3				
2016	MIN	MLB	31	1.23	3.15	5.06	-0.1	95.2	87.8	7.5	49.4
2017	MIN	MLB	32	1.15	2.78	4.76	0.2	95.1	80.9	6.5	46.9
2017	WAS	MLB	32	1.15	3.46	5.84	-0.2	94.7	83.2	4.8	54.7
2018	WAS	MLB	33	1.24	3.59	6.36	-0.7	93.9	83.6	7.4	48.9
2018	CHN	MLB	33	2.00	7.00	6.40	-0.3	94.5	85.8	8.4	45.4
2019	CHN	MLB	34	1.49	5.16	5.05	-0.1	93.5	82.8	6.9	48

Chicago Cubs 2019

Brandon Kintzler, continued

Pitch Shape vs LHH

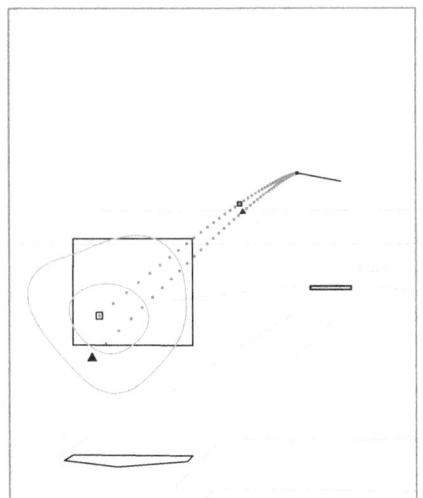

Pitch Shape vs RHH

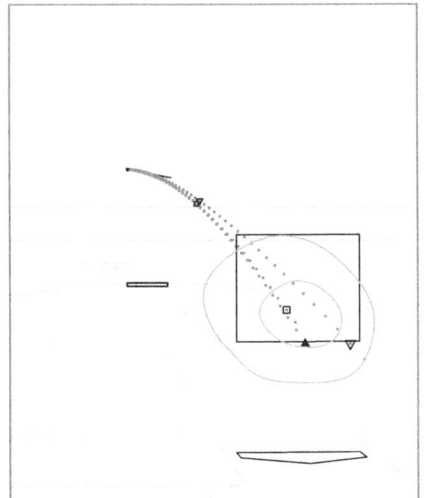

Type	Frequency	Velocity	H Movement	V Movement
● Fastball	4.2%	93.2 [102]	-6.9 [99]	-16 [99]
☐ Sinker	80.2%	93 [103]	-13.1 [96]	-19.3 [103]
+ Cutter				
▲ Changeup	7.4%	88.4 [112]	-14.3 [84]	-22.8 [114]
✕ Splitter				
▽ Slider	8.2%	87.1 [112]	0.1 [79]	-28.8 [113]
◇ Curveball				
⊕ Slow Curveball				
✳ Knuckleball				
▼ Screwball				

Jon Lester   LHP

Born: 01/07/84   Age: 35   Bats: L   Throws: L
Height: 6'4"   Weight: 240   Origin: Round 2, 2002 Draft (#57 overall)

YEAR	TEAM	LVL	AGE	W	L	SV	G	GS	IP	H	HR	BB/9	K/9	K	GB%	BABIP
2016	CHN	MLB	32	19	5	0	32	32	202^2	154	21	2.3	8.7	197	48%	.256
2017	CHN	MLB	33	13	8	0	32	32	180^2	179	26	3.0	9.0	180	48%	.310
2018	CHN	MLB	34	18	6	0	32	32	181^2	174	24	3.2	7.4	149	40%	.290
2019	CHN	MLB	35	10	11	0	29	29	174	173	25	2.9	7.9	153	44%	.294

Breakout: 20%   Improve: 41%   Collapse: 25%   Attrition: 12%   MLB: 93%
Comparables: Jeff Fassero, Koji Uehara, John Smoltz

Another year, another 30-plus starts for Lester. 2018 took his annual streak of at least 31 starts to eleven, a number only two other active pitchers (Justin Verlander and James Shields) have reached at all, let alone consecutively. Despite the ERA, this was far from a vintage performance. The diminished innings total from 2017 was almost exactly replicated, only this time with a huge decline in strikeouts and grounders. Lester's primary whiff-inducing pitches, the changeup and curveball, both missed fewer bats than at any point since he arrived in Chicago. On the plus side, his well-documented inability to control the running game is barely an issue now with Willson Contreras behind the plate: for the second straight year, 39 percent of thieves were caught in the act with Lester on the mound, and he even picked off another runner for good measure. It seems increasingly likely that day Lester doesn't reach 30 starts will come only when he decides to hang up his cleats for good.

YEAR	TEAM	LVL	AGE	WHIP	ERA	DRA	WARP	MPH	FB%	WHF	CSP
2016	CHN	MLB	32	1.02	2.44	2.77	6.0	94.4	58.5	11.2	44.3
2017	CHN	MLB	33	1.32	4.33	3.71	3.8	92.7	50.6	11.3	42
2018	CHN	MLB	34	1.31	3.32	4.44	1.8	92.5	50.3	8.9	47
2019	CHN	MLB	35	1.32	4.43	4.59	0.9	91.9	51.5	10.1	43.8

Jon Lester, continued

Pitch Shape vs LHH

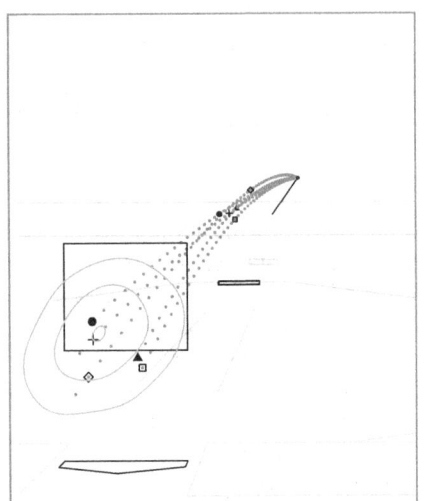

Pitch Shape vs RHH

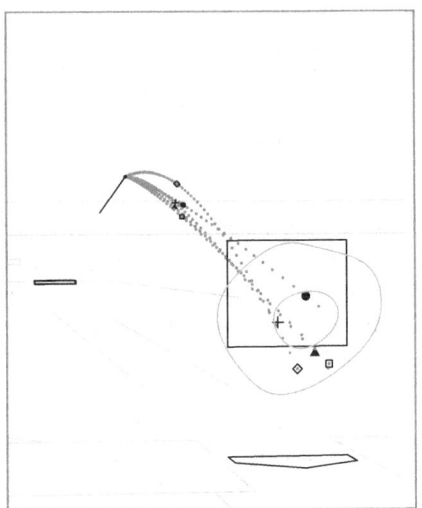

Type	Frequency	Velocity	H Movement	V Movement
● Fastball	45.3%	91.5 [97]	7.2 [98]	-15.1 [102]
☐ Sinker	5.0%	90.6 [91]	12.6 [100]	-23.2 [91]
+ Cutter	24.7%	88.5 [98]	-1.1 [96]	-21.7 [108]
▲ Changeup	9.3%	85.4 [100]	12.8 [92]	-28.2 [97]
✕ Splitter				
▽ Slider				
◇ Curveball	15.7%	75.1 [88]	-9.6 [108]	-48 [100]
⊕ Slow Curveball				
✳ Knuckleball				
▼ Screwball				

Dillon Maples RHP

Born: 05/09/92 Age: 27 Bats: R Throws: R
Height: 6'2" Weight: 225 Origin: Round 14, 2011 Draft (#429 overall)

YEAR	TEAM	LVL	AGE	W	L	SV	G	GS	IP	H	HR	BB/9	K/9	K	GB%	BABIP
2016	MYR	A+	24	0	1	0	9	0	7	9	0	9.0	7.7	6	69%	.346
2016	SBN	A	24	1	2	9	19	0	25	18	1	3.6	6.1	17	76%	.233
2017	MYR	A+	25	4	0	3	21	0	31^1	21	2	4.3	12.6	44	65%	.288
2017	TEN	AA	25	1	1	6	14	0	13^2	11	0	7.2	18.4	28	64%	.440
2017	IOW	AAA	25	1	2	4	17	0	18^1	12	1	5.4	13.7	28	63%	.297
2017	CHN	MLB	25	0	0	0	6	0	5^1	6	0	10.1	18.6	11	50%	.600
2018	IOW	AAA	26	2	3	10	41	0	38^2	22	1	9.1	17.5	75	57%	.350
2018	CHN	MLB	26	1	0	0	9	0	5^1	7	2	8.4	15.2	9	38%	.455
2019	CHN	MLB	27	1	1	0	19	0	20	16	1	6.6	11.7	27	53%	.303

Breakout: 11% Improve: 21% Collapse: 20% Attrition: 26% MLB: 46%
Comparables: Cesar Cabral, Jack Leathersich, Jaye Chapman

For those of the opinion that there are not enough balls in play in modern baseball, Maples represents the epitome of the problem. He was practically a two-true outcomes player at Triple-A, with 64.6 percent of the batters he faced either walking or striking out. Unfortunately, the third true outcome also showed up in his second brief major league look. For someone who gets whiffs at almost unprecedented levels, Maples has been surprisingly hittable when batters actually accomplish the rare feat of putting the ball in play against him, an issue that is tied to how much he really knows where the ball is going. A step forward in control seems to be all that separates Maples from a late-inning role, but the magnitude of that step might be even greater than his strikeout rate.

YEAR	TEAM	LVL	AGE	WHIP	ERA	DRA	WARP	MPH	FB%	WHF	CSP
2016	MYR	A+	24	2.29	7.71	6.90	-0.1				
2016	SBN	A	24	1.12	3.24	3.86	0.2				
2017	MYR	A+	25	1.15	2.01	2.57	0.9				
2017	TEN	AA	25	1.61	3.29	0.98	0.6				
2017	IOW	AAA	25	1.25	1.96	0.82	0.9				
2017	CHN	MLB	25	2.25	10.12	1.81	0.2	98.2	43.1	12.8	48.9
2018	IOW	AAA	26	1.58	2.79	0.27	2.1				
2018	CHN	MLB	26	2.25	11.81	4.86	0.0	98.0	23.9	6.3	47.5
2019	CHN	MLB	27	1.55	3.93	4.11	0.2	97.6	31.6	8.9	48.7

Chicago Cubs 2019

Dillon Maples, continued

Pitch Shape vs LHH	Pitch Shape vs RHH
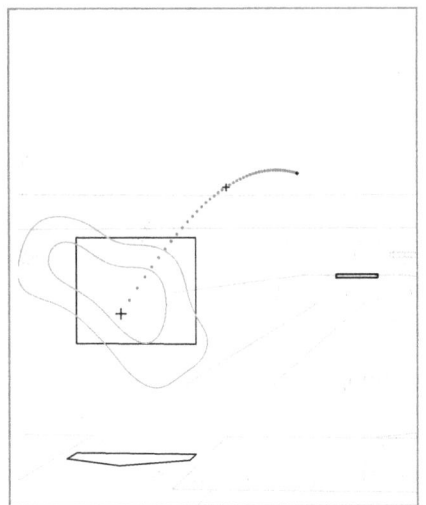	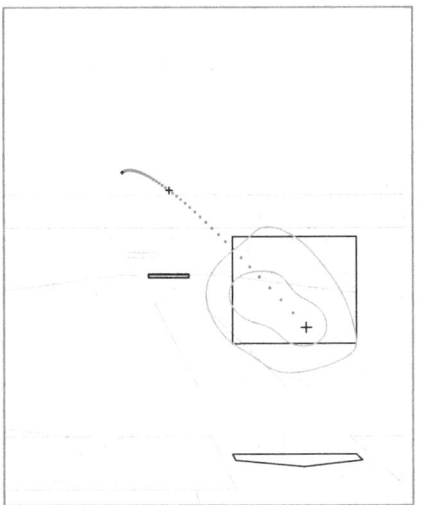

Type	Frequency	Velocity	H Movement	V Movement
● Fastball	23.9%	97.4 [116]	-2.4 [120]	-17.5 [95]
☐ Sinker				
+ Cutter	69.0%	88.4 [98]	14.4 [173]	-35.1 [54]
▲ Changeup				
✕ Splitter				
▽ Slider				
◇ Curveball	7.0%	84.1 [121]	12.4 [119]	-48 [100]
⊕ Slow Curveball				
✱ Knuckleball				
▼ Screwball				

Alec Mills   RHP
Born: 11/30/91   Age: 27   Bats: R   Throws: R
Height: 6'4"   Weight: 190   Origin: Round 22, 2012 Draft (#673 overall)

YEAR	TEAM	LVL	AGE	W	L	SV	G	GS	IP	H	HR	BB/9	K/9	K	GB%	BABIP
2016	NWA	AA	24	1	2	0	12	12	67²	57	2	1.6	9.0	68	44%	.314
2016	OMA	AAA	24	4	3	0	12	11	58	62	8	2.9	8.4	54	47%	.323
2016	KCA	MLB	24	0	0	0	3	0	3¹	3	0	13.5	10.8	4	44%	.333
2017	IOW	AAA	25	2	0	0	3	3	14	12	0	1.9	4.5	7	47%	.255
2018	IOW	AAA	26	5	12	0	23	23	124²	121	10	3.0	7.8	108	42%	.303
2018	CHN	MLB	26	0	1	0	7	2	18	11	1	3.5	11.5	23	51%	.250
2019	CHN	MLB	27	2	3	0	20	5	41	43	6	3.4	7.7	36	43%	.300

Breakout: 5%   Improve: 11%   Collapse: 32%   Attrition: 30%   MLB: 51%
Comparables: Luke Farrell, Edwar Cabrera, Tyler Pill

As a player primarily acquired for rotation depth, Mills has been called upon much less than he would have liked, especially given the issues Chicago had with their primary options. That might have something to do with the fact that his first scoreless outing of the year did not come until he made his Cubs debut as a reliever in late July. At least Mills was able to provide volume in the minors, frequently going six-plus innings, and he largely impressed in his major league work. Given that most of that work came out of the bullpen, a swingman role might be his best path to major league starts.

YEAR	TEAM	LVL	AGE	WHIP	ERA	DRA	WARP	MPH	FB%	WHF	CSP
2016	NWA	AA	24	1.02	2.39	3.73	1.1				
2016	OMA	AAA	24	1.40	4.19	3.97	0.9				
2016	KCA	MLB	24	2.40	13.50	7.15	-0.1	94.2	70.9	8.1	34.2
2017	IOW	AAA	25	1.07	3.21	5.61	0.0				
2018	IOW	AAA	26	1.30	4.84	3.78	2.5				
2018	CHN	MLB	26	1.00	4.00	2.42	0.6	92.3	58.9	12	47.1
2019	CHN	MLB	27	1.43	4.76	4.83	0.1	92.0	61.4	11.5	42.8

Alec Mills, continued

Pitch Shape vs LHH

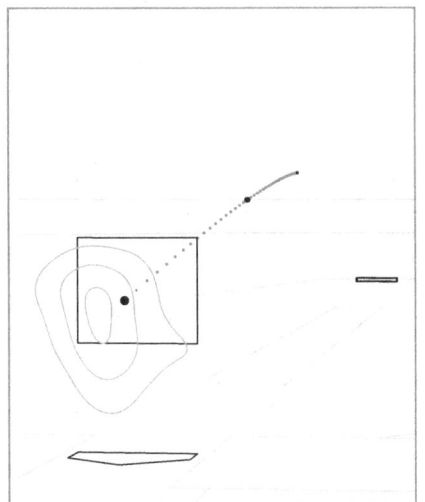

Pitch Shape vs RHH

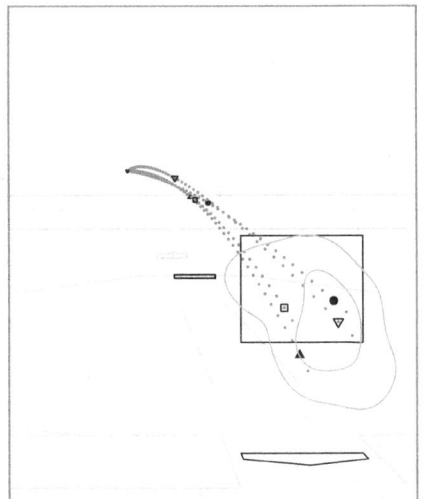

Type	Frequency	Velocity	H Movement	V Movement
● Fastball	34.6%	90.9 [95]	-8.2 [93]	-16.2 [98]
☐ Sinker	24.3%	90.7 [91]	-14.2 [87]	-22.2 [94]
+ Cutter				
▲ Changeup	19.5%	81.3 [84]	-13 [91]	-33.2 [83]
✕ Splitter				
▽ Slider	13.7%	78.6 [74]	14 [139]	-41.1 [76]
◇ Curveball	7.9%	72.1 [77]	12.3 [119]	-56.9 [80]
⊕ Slow Curveball				
✱ Knuckleball				
▼ Screwball				

Mike Montgomery LHP

Born: 07/01/89 Age: 29 Bats: L Throws: L
Height: 6'5" Weight: 215 Origin: Round 1, 2008 Draft (#36 overall)

YEAR	TEAM	LVL	AGE	W	L	SV	G	GS	IP	H	HR	BB/9	K/9	K	GB%	BABIP
2016	SEA	MLB	26	3	4	0	32	2	61^2	49	3	2.6	7.9	54	59%	.272
2016	CHN	MLB	26	1	1	0	17	5	38^1	30	5	4.7	8.9	38	61%	.258
2017	CHN	MLB	27	7	8	3	44	14	130^2	103	10	3.8	6.9	100	59%	.253
2018	CHN	MLB	28	5	6	0	38	19	124	131	10	2.8	6.2	86	53%	.309
2019	CHN	MLB	29	4	4	0	45	6	72	71	8	3.6	7.2	59	54%	.292

Breakout: 27% Improve: 53% Collapse: 20% Attrition: 14% MLB: 92%
Comparables: Jhoulys Chacin, Alex Colome, Kyle Gibson

Nineteen starts. Nineteen relief appearances. Montgomery's numbers look like those of the quintessential swingman, making spot starts when needed and providing relief innings if the regular starters were healthy. That moniker implies more role changes than Montgomery really made: he started the year with 18 relief appearances before moving into the rotation in late May, with just a solitary bullpen outing in August interrupting that string of 19 starts. Surprisingly neat split aside, he did exactly what the Cubs have him on the roster for: fill in with solid innings wherever a gap arises. Contrary to his previous results, Montgomery was much better as starter than reliever in 2018, but it doesn't seem he'll get a chance to pitch a full season in the role with the Cubs.

YEAR	TEAM	LVL	AGE	WHIP	ERA	DRA	WARP	MPH	FB%	WHF	CSP
2016	SEA	MLB	26	1.09	2.34	4.02	0.8	96.4	47.8	11.2	45.7
2016	CHN	MLB	26	1.30	2.82	2.48	1.2	95.5	47.8	13.6	45.1
2017	CHN	MLB	27	1.21	3.38	4.31	1.6	94.1	53	8.9	44.6
2018	CHN	MLB	28	1.37	3.99	4.57	0.9	93.3	49.6	9.9	49.6
2019	CHN	MLB	29	1.38	4.52	4.60	0.3	93.5	50.5	10	46.9

Mike Montgomery, continued

Pitch Shape vs LHH	Pitch Shape vs RHH
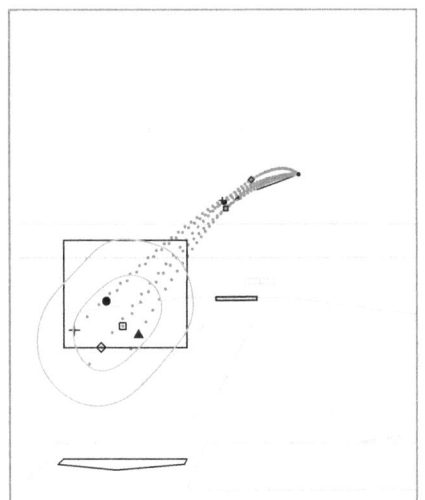	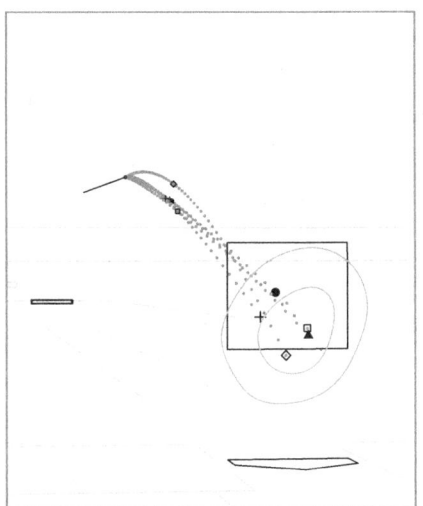

Type	Frequency	Velocity	H Movement	V Movement
● Fastball	17.3%	91.6 [97]	7.9 [94]	-18 [93]
☐ Sinker	32.3%	92.1 [98]	13.1 [96]	-20.2 [101]
+ Cutter	8.6%	88.3 [97]	4 [66]	-26 [91]
▲ Changeup	19.9%	83.5 [93]	14.3 [84]	-29.5 [94]
✕ Splitter				
▽ Slider				
◇ Curveball	21.8%	77.7 [97]	-6.4 [94]	-47.8 [101]
⊕ Slow Curveball				
✱ Knuckleball				
▼ Screwball				

Brandon Morrow RHP

Born: 07/26/84 Age: 34 Bats: R Throws: R
Height: 6'3" Weight: 205 Origin: Round 1, 2006 Draft (#5 overall)

YEAR	TEAM	LVL	AGE	W	L	SV	G	GS	IP	H	HR	BB/9	K/9	K	GB%	BABIP
2016	LEL	A+	31	0	1	0	2	2	11²	15	1	2.3	6.2	8	41%	.368
2016	SAN	AA	31	1	1	0	2	2	10¹	18	3	3.5	3.5	4	40%	.375
2016	ELP	AAA	31	0	0	2	12	2	21	29	2	3.9	9.0	21	52%	.403
2016	SDN	MLB	31	1	0	0	18	0	16	19	2	1.7	4.5	8	47%	.309
2017	OKL	AAA	32	0	5	6	20	0	20	25	5	2.2	9.9	22	56%	.339
2017	LAN	MLB	32	6	0	2	45	0	43²	31	0	1.9	10.3	50	46%	.282
2018	CHN	MLB	33	0	0	22	35	0	30²	24	2	2.6	9.1	31	53%	.278
2019	CHN	MLB	34	2	2	20	39	0	41	39	5	3.7	8.7	40	47%	.303

Breakout: 16% Improve: 36% Collapse: 16% Attrition: 11% MLB: 70%
Comparables: Zach Duke, John Bale, Dale Thayer

It looked as though Morrow had finally done the impossible and found a role that allowed him to both stay healthy and consistently perform at the elite level he has teased us with throughout his career. Naturally, it was too good to be true. Although Morrow proved that his 2017 dominance was no fluke, he also returned to a role that he is sadly more familiar with than any other: occupying a spot on the 60-day DL.

YEAR	TEAM	LVL	AGE	WHIP	ERA	DRA	WARP	MPH	FB%	WHF	CSP
2016	LEL	A+	31	1.54	6.94	5.50	0.0				
2016	SAN	AA	31	2.13	7.84	5.42	0.0				
2016	ELP	AAA	31	1.81	6.43	4.55	0.1				
2016	SDN	MLB	31	1.38	1.69	5.03	0.0	97.1	48	11.9	50.7
2017	OKL	AAA	32	1.50	7.20	3.38	0.4				
2017	LAN	MLB	32	0.92	2.06	2.98	1.1	99.6	59.5	16.8	47.1
2018	CHN	MLB	33	1.08	1.47	3.66	0.4	99.2	72.8	14.1	48.2
2019	CHN	MLB	34	1.39	3.97	4.13	0.3	97.9	63	14.8	47.8

Chicago Cubs 2019

Brandon Morrow, continued

Pitch Shape vs LHH

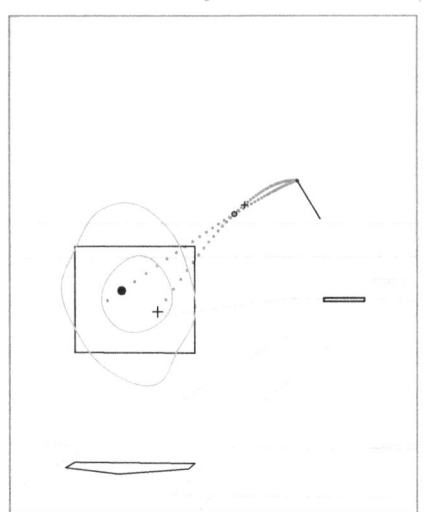

Pitch Shape vs RHH

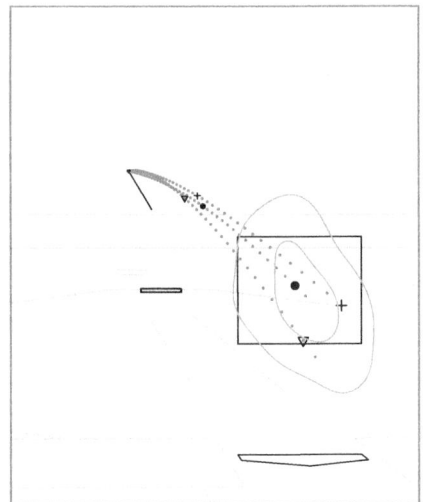

Type	Frequency	Velocity	H Movement	V Movement
● Fastball	72.7%	98.1 [118]	-9.2 [88]	-11.6 [113]
☐ Sinker				
+ Cutter	13.7%	92.5 [122]	5 [118]	-22.9 [103]
▲ Changeup				
× Splitter				
▽ Slider	13.5%	88.9 [120]	3.7 [95]	-34.4 [96]
◇ Curveball				
⊕ Slow Curveball				
✱ Knuckleball				
▼ Screwball				

James Norwood RHP

Born: 12/24/93 Age: 25 Bats: R Throws: R
Height: 6'2" Weight: 215 Origin: Round 7, 2014 Draft (#199 overall)

YEAR	TEAM	LVL	AGE	W	L	SV	G	GS	IP	H	HR	BB/9	K/9	K	GB%	BABIP
2016	SBN	A	22	3	1	6	22	0	26^2	30	0	2.7	11.8	35	47%	.400
2016	MYR	A+	22	1	0	1	8	0	9^1	12	0	1.9	7.7	8	44%	.375
2017	MYR	A+	23	3	0	6	27	0	39	32	1	3.7	9.5	41	37%	.313
2017	TEN	AA	23	1	3	1	14	0	18^2	22	1	4.3	9.2	19	46%	.362
2018	TEN	AA	24	1	2	2	25	0	32^2	25	2	3.3	9.9	36	40%	.277
2018	IOW	AAA	24	1	1	0	15	0	17^2	11	1	6.1	10.7	21	34%	.250
2018	CHN	MLB	24	0	1	0	11	0	11	14	0	4.1	8.2	10	31%	.359
2019	CHN	MLB	25	0	1	0	10	0	10^1	10	1	4.6	9.3	11	39%	.300

Breakout: 6% Improve: 10% Collapse: 6% Attrition: 9% MLB: 17%
Comparables: Chad Smith, Kevin McCarthy, Angel Nesbitt

Halfway through 2018, Norwood probably wasn't even the most famous James Norwood in sports: his British counterpart scored the goal that ensured Tranmere Rovers returned to the English Football League. If that seems like a particularly low bar to fail to clear, bear in mind that the American Norwood struggled to deal with Double-A hitters less than a year earlier and was yet to make his major league debut. The Cubs soon addressed that after his success at both Tennessee and Iowa, calling him up for a handful of games in early July and then bringing him back for good in late August. Norwood relies heavily on his big fastball, which sits 98 and touches 100, throwing it over 70 percent of the time. While that's not a terrible pitch to rely on, a lack of convincing alternatives leaves him vulnerable to hitters at the highest level.

YEAR	TEAM	LVL	AGE	WHIP	ERA	DRA	WARP	MPH	FB%	WHF	CSP
2016	SBN	A	22	1.42	3.71	2.10	0.8				
2016	MYR	A+	22	1.50	1.93	3.18	0.2				
2017	MYR	A+	23	1.23	2.31	3.14	0.8				
2017	TEN	AA	23	1.66	5.30	3.66	0.3				
2018	TEN	AA	24	1.13	2.48	3.53	0.5				
2018	IOW	AAA	24	1.30	2.55	3.88	0.3				
2018	CHN	MLB	24	1.73	4.09	5.45	-0.1	99.7	71.4	8.4	48.7
2019	CHN	MLB	25	1.52	4.97	4.91	0.0	99.4	73.1	8.6	49.9

Chicago Cubs 2019

James Norwood, continued

Pitch Shape vs LHH

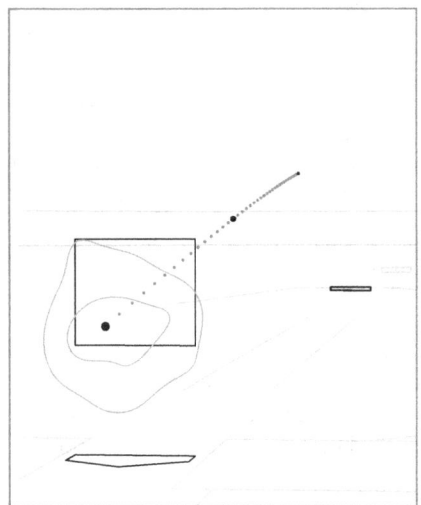

Pitch Shape vs RHH

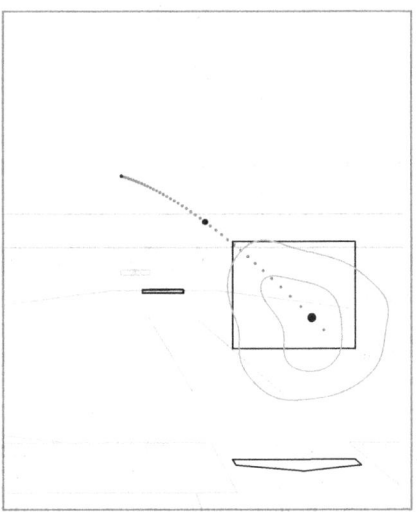

Type	Frequency	Velocity	H Movement	V Movement
● Fastball	71.4%	97.9 [117]	-8.5 [92]	-12 [112]
☐ Sinker				
+ Cutter				
▲ Changeup	13.2%	89.5 [117]	-5.3 [132]	-26.7 [102]
✕ Splitter				
▽ Slider	15.4%	85.6 [105]	2.4 [89]	-33.7 [98]
◇ Curveball				
⊕ Slow Curveball				
✳ Knuckleball				
▼ Screwball				

Jose Quintana   LHP

Born: 01/24/89   Age: 30   Bats: R   Throws: L
Height: 6'1"   Weight: 220   Origin: International Free Agent, 2006

YEAR	TEAM	LVL	AGE	W	L	SV	G	GS	IP	H	HR	BB/9	K/9	K	GB%	BABIP
2016	CHA	MLB	27	13	12	0	32	32	208	192	22	2.2	7.8	181	41%	.293
2017	CHA	MLB	28	4	8	0	18	18	104¹	98	14	3.5	9.4	109	45%	.301
2017	CHN	MLB	28	7	3	0	14	14	84¹	72	9	2.2	10.5	98	48%	.300
2018	CHN	MLB	29	13	11	0	32	32	174¹	162	25	3.5	8.2	158	45%	.282
2019	CHN	MLB	30	10	10	0	29	29	165¹	158	20	3.1	8.6	159	43%	.297

Breakout: 5%   Improve: 37%   Collapse: 34%   Attrition: 10%   MLB: 96%
Comparables: Gavin Floyd, Yovani Gallardo, Gaylord Perry

You know when you keep telling someone how good something is, and then when they finally try it, it's just not quite right? A different chef was working the day you went back to a restaurant, the drink you tried on the beach on vacation just doesn't taste the same in your backyard, the band who blew you away in a small venue are underwhelming in an arena. For years, Quintana's talents went rather underappreciated on a White Sox team that never finished better than fourth in any of his full seasons, although Cubs fans got a half-season glimpse of the talent before a 2017 NLCS implosion. Finally given a whole campaign to showcase his talents on the North Side for the division favorites, Quintana had the worst season of his career, frequently losing his trademark command and getting crushed the third time through the order. Even if it's just for one year, it would be nice if Quintana was exactly as good as you've been telling everyone.

YEAR	TEAM	LVL	AGE	WHIP	ERA	DRA	WARP	MPH	FB%	WHF	CSP
2016	CHA	MLB	27	1.16	3.20	4.13	2.9	94.6	66.8	8.5	47.7
2017	CHA	MLB	28	1.32	4.49	4.59	1.1	93.3	62.2	9.3	44.7
2017	CHN	MLB	28	1.10	3.74	3.94	1.5	94.0	63.7	9.3	46.4
2018	CHN	MLB	29	1.32	4.03	4.93	0.8	93.2	68.3	8.8	49
2019	CHN	MLB	30	1.30	4.01	4.14	1.8	93.0	65.8	8.9	47.3

Chicago Cubs 2019

Jose Quintana, continued

Pitch Shape vs LHH **Pitch Shape vs RHH**

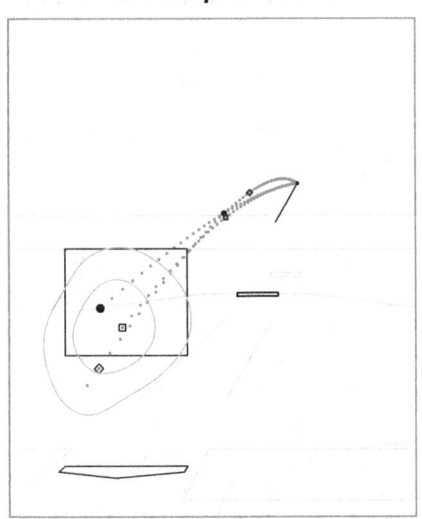 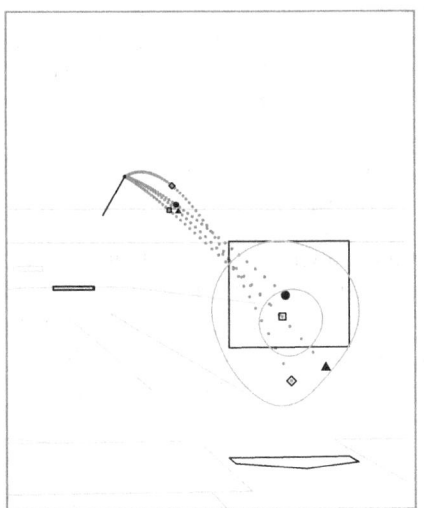

Type	Frequency	Velocity	H Movement	V Movement
● Fastball	50.2%	92 [98]	5 [108]	-14.5 [104]
□ Sinker	18.0%	92 [98]	11.8 [107]	-16.9 [111]
+ Cutter				
▲ Changeup	6.8%	86.8 [106]	9.7 [109]	-26.3 [103]
× Splitter				
▽ Slider				
◇ Curveball	24.9%	76.5 [93]	-5.9 [92]	-49.9 [96]
⊕ Slow Curveball				
✶ Knuckleball				
▼ Screwball				

Randy Rosario LHP

Born: 05/18/94 Age: 25 Bats: L Throws: L
Height: 6'1" Weight: 200 Origin: International Free Agent, 2010

YEAR	TEAM	LVL	AGE	W	L	SV	G	GS	IP	H	HR	BB/9	K/9	K	GB%	BABIP
2016	FTM	A+	22	6	6	1	21	16	94^1	102	3	3.2	6.5	68	58%	.330
2016	CHT	AA	22	0	1	0	4	0	6	6	1	7.5	15.0	10	50%	.385
2017	MIN	MLB	23	0	0	0	2	0	2^1	7	1	0.0	7.7	2	67%	.545
2017	CHT	AA	23	1	0	1	32	0	57^1	57	4	3.6	7.1	45	51%	.312
2018	IOW	AAA	24	0	0	0	15	0	22^2	13	1	2.4	6.0	15	48%	.190
2018	CHN	MLB	24	4	0	1	44	0	46^2	47	5	4.2	5.8	30	53%	.294
2019	CHN	MLB	25	1	1	0	24	0	25^2	27	3	4.4	7.2	21	49%	.300

Breakout: 23% Improve: 34% Collapse: 26% Attrition: 44% MLB: 67%
Comparables: Enrique Gonzalez, Dovydas Neverauskas, Zach Miner

Rosario keeps the infield grass well-trimmed with his four-seam/sinker/slider combo, all of which induce grounders at an above-average rate. It's a contact-focused profile that's tough on worms and left-handed hitters alike. Righties feel considerably more comfortable, a problem present throughout the minors and exacerbated by major-league competition, where an .876 OPS against sums up Rosario's struggles. He has toyed with incorporating a changeup, which would go a long way towards addressing such issues, although it is far from ready to feature on a regular basis. Until such an improvement is made, he realistically remains a lefty-only option unless a grounder is desperately needed and his manager is feeling lucky.

YEAR	TEAM	LVL	AGE	WHIP	ERA	DRA	WARP	MPH	FB%	WHF	CSP
2016	FTM	A+	22	1.44	3.34	3.76	1.8				
2016	CHT	AA	22	1.83	10.50	2.07	0.2				
2017	MIN	MLB	23	3.00	30.86	7.34	-0.1	96.2	67.2	6.2	41.6
2017	CHT	AA	23	1.40	4.08	3.53	0.9				
2018	IOW	AAA	24	0.84	0.79	3.77	0.4				
2018	CHN	MLB	24	1.48	3.66	5.16	-0.1	95.1	60	10.3	47.9
2019	CHN	MLB	25	1.54	5.23	5.11	-0.1	94.9	61.9	10.2	46.2

Chicago Cubs 2019

Randy Rosario, continued

Pitch Shape vs LHH	Pitch Shape vs RHH
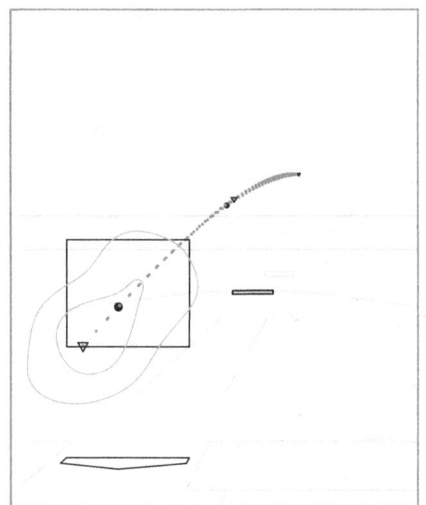	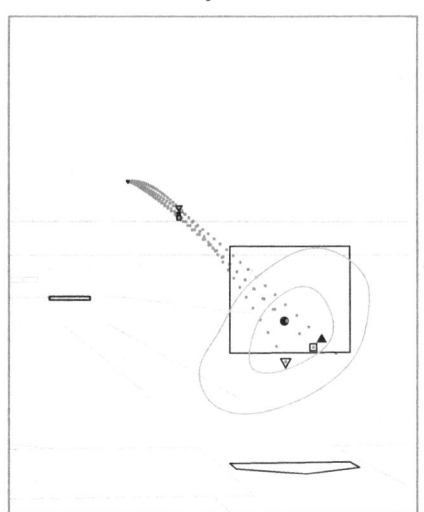

Type	Frequency	Velocity	H Movement	V Movement
● Fastball	42.6%	93.8 [104]	7.3 [97]	-18.7 [91]
□ Sinker	17.4%	92.9 [102]	14 [88]	-22.1 [94]
+ Cutter				
▲ Changeup	4.2%	87.1 [107]	12.8 [92]	-24.8 [107]
× Splitter				
▽ Slider	35.8%	86.2 [108]	-2.8 [91]	-31.7 [104]
◇ Curveball				
⊕ Slow Curveball				
✳ Knuckleball				
▼ Screwball				

Pedro Strop   RHP
Born: 06/13/85   Age: 34   Bats: R   Throws: R
Height: 6'1"   Weight: 220   Origin: International Free Agent, 2002

YEAR	TEAM	LVL	AGE	W	L	SV	G	GS	IP	H	HR	BB/9	K/9	K	GB%	BABIP
2016	CHN	MLB	31	2	2	0	54	0	47¹	27	4	2.9	11.4	60	61%	.221
2017	CHN	MLB	32	5	4	0	69	0	60¹	45	4	3.9	9.7	65	61%	.270
2018	CHN	MLB	33	6	1	13	60	0	59²	38	4	3.2	8.6	57	48%	.222
2019	*CHN*	*MLB*	*34*	*2*	*3*	*10*	*49*	*0*	*51*	*45*	*6*	*3.9*	*9.0*	*51*	*52%*	*.283*

Breakout: 9%   Improve: 29%   Collapse: 44%   Attrition: 7%   MLB: 91%
Comparables: Heath Bell, Francisco Cordero, Billy Wagner

There's a legitimate case to be made that Strop is one of the best Cubs relievers of all time. Those qualifiers might veer dangerously close to 'fun' fact territory, but consider that Strop's ERA ranks second all-time among Chicago relievers with at least 100 innings pitched, behind only Hall of Famer Bruce Sutter. Or what about his 28.2 percent strikeout rate, good for third on the same list? Orioles fans do not need more reasons to feel bad about the Jake Arrieta trade, so we can gloss over the fact that Strop is one of the twenty best relievers by WARP in the last half-decade. His lowest strikeout rate since arriving in Chicago suggests that age is starting to diminish the stuff just a little, but he remains extremely difficult to square up. He'll go into 2019 looking for a sixth straight year of an ERA beginning with two.

YEAR	TEAM	LVL	AGE	WHIP	ERA	DRA	WARP	MPH	FB%	WHF	CSP
2016	CHN	MLB	31	0.89	2.85	2.32	1.4	97.0	42.4	16.4	41.8
2017	CHN	MLB	32	1.18	2.83	3.23	1.3	97.2	55.7	16.3	43.1
2018	CHN	MLB	33	0.99	2.26	3.67	0.9	96.4	38.6	17	42.7
2019	*CHN*	*MLB*	*34*	*1.28*	*4.07*	*4.23*	*0.3*	*95.6*	*45.3*	*16.3*	*41.9*

Chicago Cubs 2019

Pedro Strop, continued

Pitch Shape vs LHH

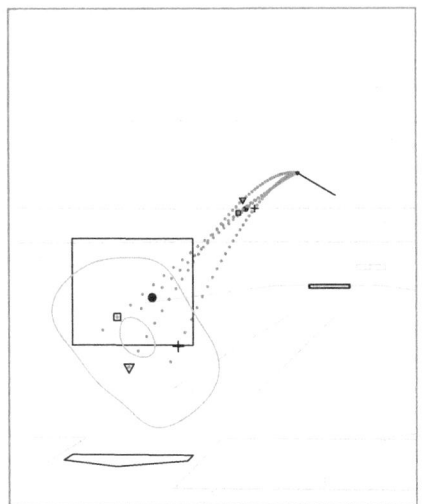

Pitch Shape vs RHH

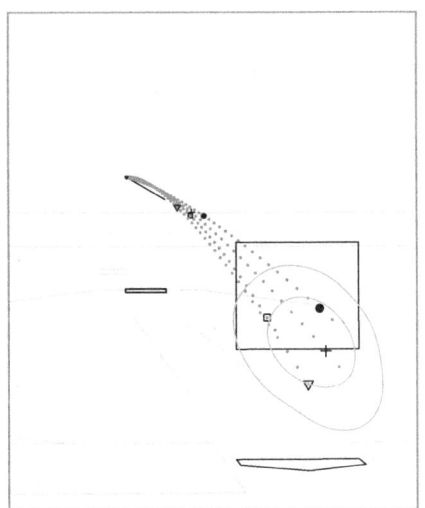

Type	Frequency	Velocity	H Movement	V Movement
● Fastball	14.7%	95.4 [109]	-4 [112]	-12.7 [110]
☐ Sinker	23.8%	95.6 [116]	-12 [105]	-16.9 [111]
+ Cutter	29.6%	89.1 [102]	2.7 [105]	-25.9 [91]
▲ Changeup				
✕ Splitter	1.8%	89.4 [120]	-6.7 [106]	-26.8 [111]
▽ Slider	30.0%	84.2 [99]	4.1 [97]	-35.5 [93]
◇ Curveball				
⊕ Slow Curveball				
✳ Knuckleball				
▼ Screwball				

Aramis Ademan SS

Born: 09/13/98 Age: 20 Bats: L Throws: R
Height: 5'11" Weight: 160 Origin: International Free Agent, 2015

YEAR	TEAM	LVL	AGE	PA	R	2B	3B	HR	RBI	BB	K	SB	CS	AVG/OBP/SLG
2016	DCH	RK	17	248	37	5	4	0	16	34	28	17	9	.254/.366/.316
2017	EUG	A-	18	183	23	9	4	4	27	14	30	10	6	.286/.365/.466
2017	SBN	A	18	134	13	6	1	3	15	4	24	4	2	.244/.269/.378
2018	MYR	A+	19	452	49	11	3	3	38	38	95	9	5	.207/.291/.273
2019	CHN	MLB	20	251	22	4	0	6	18	10	63	2	1	.151/.193/.240

Breakout: 5% Improve: 5% Collapse: 0% Attrition: 1% MLB: 5%
Comparables: Amed Rosario, Ruben Tejada, Wilfredo Tovar

If you missed the opportunity to get into Ademan before it was cool last season, you have another chance now. Granted, the Dominican shortstop was just 19 at High-A and displayed a good approach at the plate despite his other offensive struggles. Ademan has also drawn praise for his defensive skills. The chance to become an Ademan hipster still exists because of that ugly slash line, which will keep him from shooting up prospect lists. Of course, if he never really hits, it might never be cool, making him a perennial hipster dream.

YEAR	TEAM	LVL	AGE	PA	DRC+	VORP	BABIP	BRR	FRAA	WARP
2016	DCH	RK	17	248	125	12.4	.293	1.1	SS(52): -1.6	1.2
2017	EUG	A-	18	183	128	19.4	.331	-3.5	SS(38): -1.0	0.1
2017	SBN	A	18	134	72	3.0	.275	0.1	SS(29): -5.0	-0.6
2018	MYR	A+	19	452	68	1.1	.264	0.0	SS(112): -8.9	-1.5
2019	CHN	MLB	20	251	14	-16.4	.177	-0.1	SS -4	-2.2

Chicago Cubs 2019

Miguel Amaya C

Born: 03/09/99 Age: 20 Bats: R Throws: R
Height: 6'1" Weight: 185 Origin: International Free Agent, 2015

YEAR	TEAM	LVL	AGE	PA	R	2B	3B	HR	RBI	BB	K	SB	CS	AVG/OBP/SLG
2016	DCH	RK	17	242	29	12	0	1	22	21	27	9	3	.245/.344/.317
2017	EUG	A-	18	244	21	14	1	3	26	11	49	1	0	.228/.266/.338
2018	SBN	A	19	479	54	21	2	12	52	50	91	1	0	.256/.349/.403
2019	CHN	MLB	20	251	18	7	0	7	24	9	67	0	0	.146/.181/.259

Breakout: 6%   Improve: 8%   Collapse: 0%   Attrition: 5%   MLB: 8%
Comparables: Carson Kelly, Jake Bauers, Freddie Freeman

Of all the prospects in the Cubs system, Amaya's stock has risen the most over the past year. That might seem like damning with faint praise; a Futures Game appearance shows that it is anything but. An athletic backstop with the frame to handle the role, Amaya started to tap into his big raw power at South Bend without sacrificing contact. Add a strong arm and signs that he can be at least average behind the plate and it's clear the Panamanian has a rare combination of skills for a catcher that add up to at least a major league regular someday. Catcher development is smooth and uncomplicated, right?

YEAR	TEAM	LVL	AGE	PA	DRC+	VORP	BABIP	BRR	FRAA	WARP
2016	DCH	RK	17	242	120	15.3	.276	2.4	C(33): -0.1, 1B(16): 3.0	1.4
2017	EUG	A-	18	244	67	1.6	.274	-1.5	C(43): -0.5, 1B(8): -0.4	-1.0
2018	SBN	A	19	479	118	31.5	.298	0.6	C(95): 2.5, 1B(9): -0.7	2.5
2019	CHN	MLB	20	251	14	-16.1	.168	-0.5	C 0, 1B 0	-1.7

Nico Hoerner SS

Born: 05/13/97 Age: 22 Bats: R Throws: R
Height: 6'1" Weight: 200 Origin: Round 1, 2018 Draft (#24 overall)

YEAR	TEAM	LVL	AGE	PA	R	2B	3B	HR	RBI	BB	K	SB	CS	AVG/OBP/SLG
2018	EUG	A-	21	28	6	0	1	1	2	5	3	4	1	.318/.464/.545
2019	CHN	MLB	22	251	24	2	1	7	24	22	64	4	1	.152/.228/.266

Breakout: 13% Improve: 18% Collapse: 0% Attrition: 17% MLB: 25%
Comparables: Yamaico Navarro, Rosell Herrera, Marcus Semien

It was a little surprising to see Hoerner taken as early as 24th overall in the 2018 draft, and the Cubs first-rounder did not get much of a chance to show that the pick was justified, going down with a strained elbow ligament after just 14 pro games. The Stanford product was sent to the Arizona Fall League to make up for lost time, the first Cubs player to make that trip in his draft season since Kris Bryant. Although that might be setting expectations *a tad* high, Hoerner was one of the biggest stars in Arizona, showing the feel for hitting and excellent makeup that inspired the lofty pick. His ability to stick at short and the extent to which the power develops will determine whether he's more than an average regular at peak, but he might reach the majors even more quickly than Bryant, especially given that his service time will be less carefully…regulated.

YEAR	TEAM	LVL	AGE	PA	DRC+	VORP	BABIP	BRR	FRAA	WARP
2018	EUG	A-	21	28	170	4.1	.333	-0.5	SS(5): -0.4	0.1
2019	CHN	MLB	22	251	33	-10.3	.172	0.5	SS 0, 2B 0	-1.1

Mark Zagunis OF
Born: 02/05/93   Age: 26   Bats: R   Throws: R
Height: 6'0"   Weight: 215   Origin: Round 3, 2014 Draft (#78 overall)

YEAR	TEAM	LVL	AGE	PA	R	2B	3B	HR	RBI	BB	K	SB	CS	AVG/OBP/SLG
2016	TEN	AA	23	211	30	13	1	4	24	30	36	1	2	.302/.408/.453
2016	IOW	AAA	23	211	31	12	4	6	25	22	42	4	0	.274/.360/.486
2017	CHN	MLB	24	18	0	0	0	0	1	4	6	2	0	.000/.222/.000
2017	IOW	AAA	24	408	59	21	1	13	55	70	93	4	3	.267/.404/.455
2018	CHN	MLB	25	6	0	1	0	0	1	1	1	0	0	.400/.500/.600
2018	IOW	AAA	25	453	63	17	0	7	40	70	101	11	1	.272/.395/.375
2019	CHN	MLB	26	35	4	1	0	1	4	5	9	0	0	.200/.314/.333

Breakout: 7%   Improve: 24%   Collapse: 7%   Attrition: 28%   MLB: 51%
Comparables: Mike Baxter, Shane Peterson, Scott Van Slyke

Zagunis has a .400 on-base percentage over more than 2000 plate appearances in the minors, demonstrating both his exceptional strike-zone judgement and his inability to force the issue in any other area. The problem is further highlighted by his increasingly lengthy stay at Triple-A. With a glove that plays only in a corner outfield spot and pop that would be more acceptable in center, the rest of the profile lags considerably behind the approach at the plate. In another organization, perhaps the walks alone would have been enough to earn Zagunis an extended look in the bigs. In Chicago, all it has earned him so far is the annual chance to battle Dan Vogelbach for the most free passes in the Pacific Coast League.

YEAR	TEAM	LVL	AGE	PA	DRC+	VORP	BABIP	BRR	FRAA	WARP
2016	TEN	AA	23	211	155	11.2	.360	-2.7	LF(40): 5.4, RF(8): -1.2	1.5
2016	IOW	AAA	23	211	117	13.5	.316	0.4	RF(33): -0.2, LF(17): 0.2	0.5
2017	CHN	MLB	24	18	70	-0.9	.000	0.6	RF(4): -0.3	0.0
2017	IOW	AAA	24	408	140	24.8	.333	-1.7	LF(53): 1.1, RF(39): -3.4	1.9
2018	CHN	MLB	25	6	91	0.9	.500	0.0	RF(1): 0.0	0.0
2018	IOW	AAA	25	453	122	22.2	.353	-1.4	RF(63): -7.0, LF(44): -3.8	0.3
2019	CHN	MLB	26	35	81	0.2	.301	0.0	RF -1	-0.1

Adbert Alzolay RHP
Born: 03/01/95 Age: 24 Bats: R Throws: R
Height: 6'0" Weight: 179 Origin: International Free Agent, 2012

YEAR	TEAM	LVL	AGE	W	L	SV	G	GS	IP	H	HR	BB/9	K/9	K	GB%	BABIP
2016	SBN	A	21	9	4	0	22	20	120^1	119	9	2.1	6.1	81	44%	.292
2017	MYR	A+	22	7	1	0	15	15	81^2	65	8	2.4	8.6	78	39%	.263
2017	TEN	AA	22	0	3	0	7	7	32^2	27	0	3.3	8.3	30	36%	.297
2018	IOW	AAA	23	2	4	0	8	8	39^2	43	4	2.9	6.1	27	37%	.307
2019	CHN	MLB	24	1	1	0	15	0	15	16	3	3.5	7.4	13	38%	.293

Breakout: 3%   Improve: 3%   Collapse: 7%   Attrition: 8%   MLB: 14%
Comparables: Jason Adam, Myles Jaye, Ryan Sherriff

A lofty ranking on Cubs prospect lists last offseason seemed to be more of a curse than a blessing for many of the unknowing recipients. Alzolay was at the top of the list and started the season just one step away from the majors. Instead of making his big-league debut, he struggled with his command at Triple-A before a severe lat strain finished his season in late May. Fortunately, it is unlikely to be a curse of Billy Goat proportions. Alzolay should have to wait only until 2019 for that debut, not 2089.

YEAR	TEAM	LVL	AGE	WHIP	ERA	DRA	WARP	MPH	FB%	WHF	CSP
2016	SBN	A	21	1.22	4.34	3.62	2.0				
2017	MYR	A+	22	1.07	2.98	3.56	1.6				
2017	TEN	AA	22	1.19	3.03	4.08	0.4				
2018	IOW	AAA	23	1.41	4.76	4.19	0.6				
2019	CHN	MLB	24	1.42	5.45	5.26	-0.1				

Chicago Cubs 2019

Jen-Ho Tseng   RHP
Born: 10/03/94   Age: 24   Bats: L   Throws: R
Height: 6'1"   Weight: 210   Origin: International Free Agent, 2013

YEAR	TEAM	LVL	AGE	W	L	SV	G	GS	IP	H	HR	BB/9	K/9	K	GB%	BABIP
2016	TEN	AA	21	6	8	0	22	22	113^1	138	12	2.5	5.5	69	49%	.327
2017	TEN	AA	22	7	3	0	15	15	90^1	79	7	2.4	8.3	83	41%	.281
2017	IOW	AAA	22	6	1	0	9	9	55	48	5	2.3	6.4	39	55%	.264
2017	CHN	MLB	22	1	0	0	2	1	6	5	2	3.0	12.0	8	33%	.231
2018	CHN	MLB	23	0	0	0	1	1	2	4	1	0.0	13.5	3	57%	.500
2018	IOW	AAA	23	2	15	0	26	26	136^1	159	20	2.9	7.6	115	50%	.327
2019	CHN	MLB	24	1	1	0	3	3	15	15	2	2.9	7.4	12	46%	.295

Breakout: 8%   Improve: 21%   Collapse: 13%   Attrition: 33%   MLB: 43%
Comparables: Chad Jenkins, Richard Bleier, Nick Tepesch

After his first run through the Pacific Coast League, Tseng must have wondered what all the fuss was about. He found out in unpleasant fashion during his second attempt. Many current major-league contributors have failed to conquer the PCL and its offensive demons, so Tseng's misfortune does not automatically condemn him to failure in the majors. It does provide a stark illustration of both the tightrope command-first types like Tseng have to walk and the risks of allowing so many balls in play, particularly in hitter-friendly parks. With four pitches that he can throw for strikes, including a plus change, a role as a number four or five is still realistic. There's a temptation to point to another command-first starter on this roster who is far more than simply the sum of his parts, but a huge spectrum of outcomes lies between not being able to start in the majors and Kyle Hendricks. Tseng could end up in the former category and although he certainly won't be the latter, the heights of his command will dictate exactly how far along that spectrum he moves, if at all.

YEAR	TEAM	LVL	AGE	WHIP	ERA	DRA	WARP	MPH	FB%	WHF	CSP
2016	TEN	AA	21	1.50	4.29	3.59	2.0				
2017	TEN	AA	22	1.14	2.99	2.96	2.4				
2017	IOW	AAA	22	1.13	1.80	3.51	1.3				
2017	CHN	MLB	22	1.17	7.50	5.20	0.0	93.5	51.9	11.3	44.2
2018	CHN	MLB	23	2.00	13.50	2.19	0.1	91.8	53.9	17.9	45.2
2018	IOW	AAA	23	1.49	6.27	3.87	2.6				
2019	CHN	MLB	24	1.34	4.32	4.48	0.1	92.8	54.1	13.8	46.1

Duane Underwood RHP

Born: 07/20/94 Age: 24 Bats: R Throws: R
Height: 6'2" Weight: 210 Origin: Round 2, 2012 Draft (#67 overall)

YEAR	TEAM	LVL	AGE	W	L	SV	G	GS	IP	H	HR	BB/9	K/9	K	GB%	BABIP
2016	TEN	AA	21	0	5	0	13	13	58^2	66	7	4.8	7.1	46	48%	.317
2016	SBN	A	21	0	1	0	3	3	8^2	5	0	4.2	12.5	12	44%	.278
2017	TEN	AA	22	13	7	0	25	24	138	130	13	3.3	6.4	98	45%	.282
2018	CHN	MLB	23	0	1	0	1	1	4	2	1	6.8	6.8	3	50%	.111
2018	IOW	AAA	23	4	10	0	27	20	119^1	127	8	2.8	7.9	105	44%	.334
2019	CHN	MLB	24	1	2	0	17	2	25	25	4	3.9	7.9	22	43%	.295

Breakout: 12% Improve: 20% Collapse: 11% Attrition: 29% MLB: 37%
Comparables: Anthony Ranaudo, Shawn Morimando, Williams Perez

For some time, there have been suggestions that Underwood might be better off in the bullpen, where his fastball could play up and his inconsistency represents less of an issue. After an unremarkable few months of starting at Triple-A, that transition finally happened, with his final seven appearances coming in relief. While Underwood's results weren't better in that small sample, it's one sign that the team might finally share that opinion. The fact that his major league debut was also the only start he made in 2018 despite several opportunities arising in Chicago is another hint that his prospects as a starter are fading.

YEAR	TEAM	LVL	AGE	WHIP	ERA	DRA	WARP	MPH	FB%	WHF	CSP
2016	TEN	AA	21	1.65	4.91	3.67	1.0				
2016	SBN	A	21	1.04	2.08	2.35	0.3				
2017	TEN	AA	22	1.30	4.43	3.98	1.9				
2018	CHN	MLB	23	1.25	2.25	7.98	-0.1	94.8	53.3	5.2	46.1
2018	IOW	AAA	23	1.37	4.53	3.75	2.4				
2019	CHN	MLB	24	1.42	4.90	4.91	0.0	94.6	54.8	5.3	47.5

Chicago Cubs 2019

LINEOUTS

Hitters

HITTER	POS	TEAM	LVL	AGE	PA	R	2B	3B	HR	RBI	BB	K	SB	CS	AVG/OBP/SLG	DRC+	WARP
Jim Adduci	LF	TOL	AAA	33	296	39	22	1	7	44	22	60	8	1	.309/.358/.474	136	1.2
	LF	DET	MLB	33	185	19	8	2	3	21	6	45	1	0	.267/.290/.386	75	-0.9
Francisco Arcia	C	SLC	AAA	28	168	18	3	2	3	26	11	25	2	1	.283/.352/.393	81	-0.3
	C	ANA	MLB	28	106	10	5	0	6	23	1	27	1	0	.204/.226/.427	81	0.0
Brennen Davis	CF	CUT	Rk	18	72	9	2	0	0	3	10	12	6	1	.298/.431/.333	160	0.3
Taylor Davis	C	IOW	AAA	28	409	38	18	0	4	41	40	57	0	2	.275/.348/.360	106	1.7
	C	CHN	MLB	28	6	0	0	0	0	2	0	1	0	0	.400/.333/.400	90	0.0
Donald Dewees	CF	NWA	AA	24	310	35	12	5	2	25	20	48	8	4	.253/.305/.351	76	0.0
	CF	OMA	AAA	24	241	31	11	3	6	29	15	45	8	2	.266/.315/.423	94	1.5
Phillip Evans	UT	LVG	AAA	25	245	34	8	1	14	39	21	42	4	3	.256/.327/.493	85	-0.3
	UT	NYN	MLB	25	23	1	0	0	0	1	2	8	1	0	.143/.217/.143	74	0.0
Johnny Field	RF	TBA	MLB	26	179	20	9	0	6	14	7	58	4	0	.213/.253/.373	75	0.0
	RF	DUR	AAA	26	40	6	3	0	0	4	2	7	1	1	.351/.400/.432	96	0.0
	RF	ROC	AAA	26	40	1	1	0	0	1	2	8	1	0	.135/.200/.162	99	0.0
	RF	MIN	MLB	26	54	8	4	0	3	7	0	14	0	0	.250/.259/.500	76	-0.1
Cole Roederer	CF	CUT	Rk	18	161	30	4	4	5	24	18	37	13	4	.275/.354/.465	124	0.3
Zack Short	SS	TEN	AA	23	524	68	28	2	17	59	82	136	8	3	.227/.356/.417	129	3.4
D.J. Wilson	CF	MYR	A+	21	272	27	9	2	1	13	32	71	10	6	.219/.315/.287	80	-0.2

Has this ever happened to you? Is your team 20 games out of first place in July and your roster is in dire need of a nap? You've tried the rest, now try starting **Jim Adduci** at first base for a while. ⓥ **Francisco Arcia** finally got the call after twelve minor-league seasons to backfill the Martin Maldonado trade. His major league-hitting and catching skills demonstrated why it took twelve seasons. ⓥ Second-round pick **Brennen Davis** helped his high school basketball team to an Arizona state championship in his junior year, so his profile is everything one might expect: tall, athletic, toolsy and filled with enough questions about the bat that the rest could be irrelevant. ⓥ **Taylor Davis** must have taken his eyes off you this season, as he has at least one on Theo Epstein, confessing his desire to move into the front office after his career is over. His solid approach and framing acumen might just be enough to make that a long-term goal rather than an imminent career move. ⓥ It's not optimal to be a fringy fourth-outfielder in a system particularly deep in fourth outfielders. **Donnie Dewees** offers a little bit of everything—power, speed, hit—but as you read that sentence to yourself, put the stress on the "little bit" rather than the "everything." ⓥ Over the last few years, the Mets have had a habit of losing fringy middle infielders on hard takeout slides. This year, it was utility dude **Phil Evans** who followed in Ruben Tejada's unfortunate footsteps, and it wouldn't surprise us if the rest of his pro career goes about as well as Tejada's has. ⓥ **Johnny Field** has the name, modestly toolsy profile and utter lack of control over the strike zone of someone going far out of their way to be a forgettable fringe outfielder. ⚾ Not content with one high school center fielder in the second round, the Cubs grabbed a second in **Cole Roederer**. He's following in some impressive recent footsteps: five Hart High School alumni played in the majors in 2018 alone, including Trevor Bauer. ⚾ Nominative determinism is on **Zack Short's** side, unlike his Double-A strikeout rate. He can definitely play short, and the on-base skills, power, and above-average performance at every level all point towards a future major league contributor, even if the batting average comes up a little…short. ⚾ As an outfield prospect with speed as his carrying tool, the onus has been on **D.J. Wilson** to show that he's more than a set of wheels with a future as a fourth outfielder. Injuries and poor performance have kept that tag dragging in the dust behind him.

Chicago Cubs 2019

Pitchers

PITCHER	TEAM	LVL	AGE	W	L	SV	G	GS	IP	H	HR	BB/9	K/9	K	GB%	WHIP	ERA	DRA	WARP
Cory Abbott	SBN	A	22	4	1	0	9	9	47^1	35	5	2.5	10.8	57	39%	1.01	2.47	2.86	1.3
	MYR	A+	22	4	5	0	13	13	67^2	59	3	3.5	9.8	74	46%	1.26	2.53	4.94	0.3
Jose Albertos	SBN	A	19	0	5	0	9	4	13	17	1	22.2	11.8	17	51%	3.77	18.69	6.01	-0.2
	EUG	A-	19	0	4	0	11	6	17^1	19	0	17.1	10.9	21	65%	3.00	11.94	6.78	-0.3
Xavier Cedeno	CHR	AAA	31	0	0	0	20	0	21^2	12	1	1.7	10.4	25	57%	0.74	1.25	2.94	0.5
	CHA	MLB	31	2	0	1	33	0	25^1	19	1	4.6	9.9	28	55%	1.26	2.84	2.17	0.8
	MIL	MLB	31	0	0	0	15	0	8	7	0	3.4	6.8	6	52%	1.25	1.12	3.12	0.2
Ian Clarkin	WNS	A+	23	0	0	0	4	0	7^2	4	0	3.5	7.0	6	58%	0.91	2.35	3.94	0.1
	BIR	AA	23	4	5	0	18	10	68^2	74	7	4.1	4.6	35	52%	1.53	4.98	7.87	-2.1
Trevor Clifton	TEN	AA	23	3	4	0	12	12	56^2	41	0	3.7	7.1	45	36%	1.13	2.86	6.63	-0.8
	IOW	AAA	23	4	3	0	14	12	69^1	65	8	3.8	7.3	56	38%	1.36	3.89	4.11	1.1
Oscar De La Cruz	TEN	AA	23	6	7	0	16	16	77^1	76	8	3.6	8.5	73	36%	1.38	5.24	5.09	0.2
Danny Hultzen	CUB	Rk	28	0	0	0	8	3	6^2	6	1	2.7	20.2	15	27%	1.20	5.40	-0.29	0.4
Alex Lange	MYR	A+	22	6	8	0	23	23	120^1	104	6	2.8	7.6	101	45%	1.18	3.74	3.78	2.2
Brendon Little	SBN	A	21	5	11	0	22	21	101^1	106	8	3.8	8.0	90	49%	1.47	5.15	5.40	-0.2
Brailyn Marquez	EUG	A-	19	1	4	0	10	10	47^2	46	5	2.6	9.8	52	52%	1.26	3.21	3.05	1.2
	SBN	A	19	0	0	0	2	2	7	7	0	2.6	9.0	7	33%	1.29	2.57	3.54	0.1
Colin Rea	SAN	AA	27	0	3	0	6	6	24	32	3	4.9	7.9	21	39%	1.88	7.12	3.98	0.4
	ELP	AAA	27	3	2	0	12	9	51^1	58	11	4.0	8.6	49	44%	1.58	5.08	4.84	0.4
Michael Rucker	TEN	AA	24	9	6	0	26	26	132^2	111	17	2.6	8.0	118	39%	1.12	3.73	4.09	1.9
Justin Steele	CUB	Rk	22	0	0	0	5	5	18^1	9	1	2.0	13.3	27	43%	0.71	1.47	1.42	0.9
	MYR	A+	22	2	1	0	4	4	18^1	12	0	2.9	9.3	19	41%	0.98	2.45	4.03	0.3
	TEN	AA	22	0	1	0	2	2	10	8	1	2.7	6.3	7	32%	1.10	3.60	3.68	0.2
Junichi Tazawa	MIA	MLB	32	1	1	0	22	0	20	28	6	5.8	10.8	24	24%	2.05	9.00	5.84	-0.2
	TOL	AAA	32	0	1	0	7	0	7^2	11	1	5.9	11.7	10	26%	2.09	9.39	6.40	-0.1
	SLC	AAA	32	0	1	2	7	0	6^1	10	1	2.8	7.1	5	44%	1.89	7.11	4.74	0.0
	ANA	MLB	32	0	0	0	9	0	8	7	1	3.4	4.5	4	36%	1.25	2.25	7.24	-0.2
Keegan Thompson	MYR	A+	23	3	3	0	12	12	67^2	49	6	1.7	8.1	61	36%	0.92	3.19	3.65	1.3
	TEN	AA	23	6	3	0	13	13	62	66	3	3.0	7.8	54	36%	1.40	4.06	4.53	0.6
Erich Uelmen	SBN	A	22	5	5	0	11	11	56^1	54	0	2.4	9.3	58	67%	1.22	3.51	3.62	1.1
	MYR	A+	22	3	3	0	10	9	33	38	3	4.1	6.5	24	51%	1.61	4.36	4.12	0.5
Jerry Vasto	COL	MLB	26	0	0	0	1	0	0^2	3	0	13.5	13.5	1	25%	6.00	40.50	11.78	-0.1
	ABQ	AAA	26	2	1	3	37	0	37	32	3	4.4	10.7	44	46%	1.35	3.16	4.44	0.3
	KCA	MLB	26	0	1	0	5	0	3^2	3	1	2.5	7.4	3	18%	1.09	2.45	5.42	0.0
Allen Webster	CHN	MLB	28	1	0	0	3	0	3	2	1	3.0	9.0	3	33%	1.00	6.00	3.00	0.1
Rowan Wick	SAN	AA	25	2	4	5	29	0	31^1	22	0	6.0	12.1	42	58%	1.37	3.16	3.10	0.7
	ELP	AAA	25	2	0	9	20	0	22^2	16	3	4.0	8.7	22	48%	1.15	1.99	4.71	0.1

Chicago Cubs 2019

PITCHER	TEAM	LVL	AGE	W	L	SV	G	GS	IP	H	HR	BB/9	K/9	K	GB%	WHIP	ERA	DRA	WARP
Rob Zastryzny	SDN	MLB	25	0	1	0	10	0	8^1	13	1	1.1	7.6	7	43%	1.68	6.48	4.10	0.1
	CHN	MLB	26	1	0	0	6	0	5^2	6	0	6.4	4.8	3	44%	1.76	4.76	5.81	-0.1
	IOW	AAA	26	3	2	0	33	1	56	47	5	4.5	8.0	50	58%	1.34	3.86	4.04	0.7

Three months before he was drafted, **Cory Abbott** pitched the first perfect game in Loyola Marymount history. While his pro career has not been quite that impeccable, he is yet to find a level to truly challenge him. ⓧ Yes, **Jose Albertos** really went from consensus top-five prospect in this system to "oh my god that's his WHIP not his ERA" in just one season, and his continued presence on the mound throughout the season suggests the issue is mechanical, mental or both. ⓧ It's stunning that someone with strikeout and ground-ball totals as strong as **Xavier Cedeno** has worked for four different teams in as many years. In an alternate universe, those peripherals made the 86 mph cutter specialist a relief ace. ⓧ A very prudent addition to the 40-man before 2018, recording more walks than strikeouts in Double-A Birmingham before he hit the disabled list with a groin strain in May was probably as deleterious for **Ian Clarkin's** hopes of starting as the missed development time. Scouts still like his curveball. ⓧ **Trevor Clifton** went from fourth on the Cubs prospect list after 2016 to vanishing completely following a woeful 2017, but he did halt the precipitous decline in his stock with a respectable showing at Triple-A and should be given a shot at a major league job in 2019. ⓧ Staying on the field has been a problem for **Oscar De La Cruz**. Until 2018 this was entirely an injury-based problem, so pitching an uninterrupted half-season before testing positive for a masking agent and promptly being suspended represents a step forward, for the glass half-full kind of person at least. ⓧ Signed at just 16, Venezuelan righty **Richard Gallardo** possesses a plus fastball, promising curveball and changeup and the kind of command that would be the envy of prospects several years his senior. ⓧ A move to the bullpen in 2017 provided the impetus for **Justin Hancock** to finally make his major league debut, seven years after he was drafted. His fastball now sits at 96 and touches 100, or at least it did before shoulder inflammation landed him on the DL in June. ⓧ Choosing a single poster boy for TINSTAAPP would be impossible, but **Danny Hultzen** would get his own month on the 2019 calendar. The former top prospect is still working to make it to the majors, the better part of a decade after he was drafted. ⓧ 2017 first-rounder **Alex Lange** had a rather average line that conceals a season of two halves. Through ten starts at High-A, he produced a 2.89 ERA and 45 strikeouts to just ten walks, while the next thirteen saw that strikeout-walk ratio halved and a 4.41 ERA. Combined, they still point to a likely back-end starter or bullpen role. ⓧ Seven of **Brendon Little**'s 22 starts were scoreless. Six of the remaining 15 saw him give up five or more earned runs, which is how his ERA also ended up starting with five. ⓧ As a 19-year-old lefty with a fastball that touches 98, **Brailyn Marquez** handled short-season ball in impressive fashion and was promoted to South Bend late in the year as a result. He throws both four- and two-seam fastballs and flashes with his curveball, although inconsistency is to be expected given his inexperience. Ⓑ It would have been almost impossible for **Cory Mazzoni** to increase his major league ERA, as he came into the season at 17.28, but another season like 2018 and he'll finally be back in the single digits. Ⓑ **Colin Rea**, famous for being untraded from the Marlins, left a little of his right elbow behind. His rehab from Tommy John proved unsuccessful, and now he'll have to find his form and his income at the same time. Ⓑ **Michael Rucker** successfully built on his 2017 transition from the bullpen to the starting rotation, developing his changeup and curve to back up a fastball that can hit 96 at times. Ⓑ The White Sox called up **Rob Scahill** in September, narrowly pushing his streak of major league seasons to seven, despite less than 150 career innings pitched. Number eight might be his toughest challenge yet. Ⓑ It would be better if **Justin Steele** was a speedy outfielder with a penchant for swiping bags. At least his recovery from Tommy John surgery was fast: it took him just 11 months to return to the mound, and he's right back on course to be a mid-rotation starter. Ⓑ **Junichi Tazawa** will always have 2013, but currently his other possessions are a suitcase and a worsening fastball. Ⓑ **Keegan Thompson** surrendered more than half of his total earned runs in just two Double-A starts. The rest were generally far more promising, although it's still not clear he has the fastball to be anything more than the name at the bottom of the depth chart. Ⓑ If you played the delivery of a side-armer on double speed, it might look a little something like **Erich Uelmen**'s. That delivery has drawn plenty of grounders in his pro career so far, with mixed results beyond the glorious aesthetics. Ⓑ As the return piece from Colorado for Drew Butera and his beloved hair flip, **Jerry Vasto** was unable to develop his own GIF-worthy moment during his short stay in Kansas City and will now compete for an bullpen spot with the Cubs, who claimed him on waivers. Ⓑ Strangely, MLB does not hand out an award for Player You Were Most Surprised To See In The Majors. If they did, it would have gone to **Allen Webster**, who briefly reappeared after a three-year absence, a spell that covered trips to Reno, Round Rock and even the KBO. Ⓑ A converted right fielder, **Rowan Wick** reached the Padres bullpen three years after switching over to the mound. He has the command you'd expect out of a right fielder, so even though he throws hard, middle relief is his ceiling. Ⓑ It's never a good sign when your major league innings total goes down every season. It's even worse when you started from 16, so **Rob Zastryzny** is hovering dangerously close to zero.

Cubs Prospects

The State of the System:
It's better at the top than it was last year, but calling the Cubs system "improved" overall is a stretch.

The Top Ten:

1 Nico Hoerner   SS   OFP: 60   Likely: 50   ETA: Late 2020
Born: 05/13/97   Age: 22   Bats: R   Throws: R   Height: 6'1"   Weight: 200
Origin: Round 1, 2018 Draft (#24 overall)

The Report: Most years there is a late first-round pick or two who pops the summer after signing, and this year it was a… Stanford infielder? Not the usual type, but Hoerner looked like he should have been one of the best college bats in the draft before an elbow injury ended his season in July. Then he went to the AFL and shockingly the #HornyforHoerner hashtag still failed to catch on despite him raking for a month in the desert, flashing advanced bat-to-ball skills, and the usual strong approach we expect from Cubs draft picks.

Hoerner may not stick at shortstop per se, but he's athletic enough to play there, and he's in the right org to make use of his potential positional versatility. The ultimate ceiling here is going to be dependent on his turning some of his present gap power into the over-the-fence variety. But this level of polish, combined with a potential plus hit tool, a good approach, and the ability to at least stand at short makes Hoerner a high-probability major-leaguer, one who both should move fast and bring decent upside to the table.

The Risks: Medium. He's a polished, athletic college bat, so this is probably closer to low than medium, but we will round up until he has a full healthy pro season.

Bret Sayre's Fantasy Take: The last 20 years of music history has led us to sink the 90s into one giant mashup of mood lighting and dark lyrics. How many people actually remember that The Verve and The Verve Pipe were actually different bands? It's true, it's just a thing that sounds made up now that we're so far removed from it. You're also probably wondering what the hell this has to do with Hoerner.

Well, those two bands were different in one major way. While they each had one hit, The Verve's album was actually quite good and underrated. On the other hand, The Verve Pipe's album was trash… Just truly unlistenable. Unfortunately for Cubs fans (and, well, me) their farm system is basically Villans incarnate. Hoerner can flat out hit and despite not having extreme utility in either homers or steals (he's a poor bet to reach 20 of either regularly), he checks in as a borderline top 101 prospect for me in dynasty formats and a second-round pick among "The Freshmen" entering pro ball this year. These other guys, though? Not so much.

2. Miguel Amaya   C
OFP: 60   Likely: 50   ETA: 2022
Born: 03/09/99   Age: 20   Bats: R   Throws: R   Height: 6'1"   Weight: 185
Origin: International Free Agent, 2015

The Report: A breakout and bright spot in a very shallow farm system, Amaya is a potential above-average two-way catching prospect. The two standout tools at present are above-average arm strength and above-average raw power. Those are two good building blocks for an everyday catcher, but both have their caveats. The arm comes with an efficient transfer, but inconsistent throwing mechanics. The receiving isn't as good as the arm, although there are positive markers for improvement given Amaya's athleticism and quick hands.

The raw power comes from natural lift and strength from the swing, and there is enough barrel control and hand/eye to project most of it getting into games. But Amaya's swing lacks lower-half engagement and he can get off-balance and out in front when he falls in love with his pull side power. He does show the makings of a strong approach, so with even an average hit tool, Amaya should offer enough on-base and pop to be at least a solid everyday catcher.

The Risks: High. He's an A-ball catcher who needs significant refinement both at and behind the plate. And as always, catchers are weird.

Bret Sayre's Fantasy Take: "Cup of Tea" as in not quite my. How many times do we need to go over this about catching prospects? If you think Amaya is going to be the one to break through and become a top-five catcher, you might not ultimately be wrong, but there are so many things that can go haywire along the way. Waiting 3-4 years for a .260/20-homer catcher is just a bad idea when you can always get someone like Welington Castillo for basically free.

3. Alex Lange   RHP
OFP: 55   Likely: 45   ETA: 2020
Born: 10/02/95   Age: 23   Bats: R   Throws: R   Height: 6'3"   Weight: 197
Origin: Round 1, 2017 Draft (#30 overall)

The Report: The first thing you notice with Lange is his potential plus curveball. When on, it has tight spin and sharp break. However, he simply throws it too much and has shown a tendency to hang it in the zone a bit just due to the sheer amount of times it leaves his hand. The fastball clocks in around 90-92 and has some movement, but he needs to incorporate it more with his curve and improve his changeup, which is clearly his third option.

There were plenty of flashes of the good Lange this season. While his somewhat quirky motion reveals the ball a bit too much before release, his curve—if paired better with his fastball—could carry him to a mid-rotation future. Keep in mind though, he is 23 and has yet to reach Double-A. While it may simply be a product of his four-year career as a college player, he needs a strong showing next season in the upper minors to make noise in this depleted system.

The Risks: High. A two-pitch pitcher at the moment, Lange needs to rely less on his curveball (despite its effectiveness) as he rises through the ranks. There is obvious potential here, but clear inconsistency with his fastball and overall control.

Bret Sayre's Fantasy Take: Mid-rotation prospects like Lange are the "Villans" of dynasty rosters everywhere unless you roster 250 farmhands or more. There's not enough swing-and-miss here for us to be super interested in a fantasy sense as he projects to be closer to an SP5 than anything else.

Adbert Alzolay   RHP   OFP: 55   Likely: 45   ETA: 2019
Born: 03/01/95   Age: 24   Bats: R   Throws: R   Height: 6'0"   Weight: 179
Origin: International Free Agent, 2012

The Report: Before a lat strain ended his season around Memorial Day, Alzolay seemed well on his way to some sort of major-league role with the big club. The lack of progression with his command and changeup are concerning, but it's difficult to read into eight starts, of course. The fastball and slider combo is still plus, although he didn't always have his usual mid-90s heat as a starter. The mid-80s slider looks like a true out pitch, most of the time. It will still get slurvy when he tries to spot it, and it's more effective as a chase pitch gloveside and down. Alzolay's athleticism on the mound is notable and between that and good arm speed on the change you can project further growth with the pitch. Given the crowded nature of the Cubs rotation though, the org might first fashion him as a fastball/slider pen arm.

The Risks: Medium. Alzolay's lat strain was ill-timed in 2018, but it shouldn't have lingering effects into 2019. However, the changeup and command will need to tighten up this season to forestall a move to the bullpen.

Bret Sayre's Fantasy Take: The starting pitcher future for Alzolay is merely a "Veneer" on the reliever material that lies underneath. On the bright side, he's likely to be in the majors this year and could contribute in ratios and strikeouts decently for a middle reliever. On the other hand, he's a reliever who is extremely unlikely to get saves.

5. Aramis Ademan   SS

OFP: 55   Likely: 45   ETA: 2021
Born: 09/13/98   Age: 20   Bats: L   Throws: R   Height: 5'11"   Weight: 160
Origin: International Free Agent, 2015

The Report: Just 20 years old, Ademan already has a quick bat that allows him to drive the ball to all fields. He didn't show that much in High-A last year, but while his results were more than a bit concerning, there's still plenty of talent under the hood.

Ademan is just 160 pounds and he looks it, but when he is able to fully extend his hands through the zone, his bat has a nice whip to it. His athleticism is obvious, as he is able to get to balls a bit beyond the range of your average High-A shortstop. His hands and actions remain a work in progress. He has room to grow, and with an open stance and clean swing, Ademan has the potential to be a serviceable MLB shortstop. That bodes well given Chicago's track record of development for middle infielders (Baez, Russell, Torres) in recent years.

The Risks: High. The tools are good, but he was pretty bad in High-A last year.

Bret Sayre's Fantasy Take: There may be more upside than hinted at during his brutal 2018 season from a fantasy standpoint as well, but shy of a potential .280 average, the rest of his fantasy ceiling is sure to "Drive You Mild."

6. Justin Steele   LHP

OFP: 55   Likely: 45
ETA: 2019 as a reliever, 2020 as a starter.
Born: 07/11/95   Age: 23   Bats: L   Throws: L   Height: 6'2"   Weight: 195
Origin: Round 5, 2014 Draft (#139 overall)

The Report: Toeing a professional mound a mere 11 months after undergoing Tommy John surgery, Steele quickly reestablished himself as one of the top arms in the Cubs system. The snarkier among you may regard that as damning with faint praise, but I'll always have kind words for a lefty with mid-90s heat and a potential plus curve. Steele could move quickly as a reliever, and the third pitch and command issues may dictate that role change eventually anyway, but I'd expect him to continue as a starter for the extra post-TJ reps if nothing else.

The power relief arsenal from the left side would tempt me, though. While the fastball doesn't move a ton, he pounds the zone with plus velocity. The curve is a tight, 1-7 breaker that he can manipulate to spot or bury. He's comfortable going backdoor or back foot with it, which covers for the lack of a real armside weapon against righties at present.

The Risks: Medium. There's still some post-TJ risks, although he looked fine in his brief 2018 appearance, and somewhat more substantial reliever risk.

Bret Sayre's Fantasy Take: I don't want to sound too much like an "Ominous Man" (though the quality of these prospects isn't helping) and yet there's little reason to believe that Steele can end up as a starting pitcher who sits above the waiver wire line in mixed leagues.

7 **Brailyn Marquez   LHP**   OFP: 50   Likely: 40   ETA: 2022
Born: 01/30/99   Age: 20   Bats: L   Throws: L   Height: 6'4"   Weight: 185
Origin: International Free Agent, 2015

The Report: If you are going to wager on any prospect outside of, oh let's say the top 200 or so, to have a significant major league career, you won't go broke betting on the lefty sitting 96-98. Absent anything else, southpaws with that kind of velocity get chances. Marquez has a bit more to recommend than just the fastball, but just a bit. It's a plus-plus fastball though, with only command issues and velocity bleed keeping it from being a top-of-the-scale offering. Lefties facing it would be forgiven if they flinched a bit given that it comes from a low-three-quarters armslot with some funk in the delivery. The change and breaking ball are both well-below-average at present, and Marquez's delivery doesn't exactly scream "average command/control projection" either. There's effort in the arm action, and it's a bit stiff overall, but the ball does come absolutely screaming out of his left hand. And that's not nothing.

The Risks: High. This profile is mostly an arm strength bet, but man it's a lot of arm strength from the left side.

Bret Sayre's Fantasy Take: His velocity is very "Real," but his fantasy value is very not real. He doesn't need to be owned in any dynasty formats.

8 **Cole Roederer   OF**   OFP: 50   Likely: 40   ETA: 2023
Born: 09/24/99   Age: 19   Bats: L   Throws: L   Height: 6'0"   Weight: 175
Origin: Round 2C, 2018 Draft (#77 overall)

The Report: Roederer is your typical "athletic Cali prep outfielder without quite loud enough tools to go in round one." Yeah, it's not as unusual a taxonomy as you might think. He has above-average bat speed, but his swing plane—especially as an amateur—was not geared for much in the way of power. The problem is that he may slow down enough to force a slide over to left field (his below-average arm won't play in the other corner). He flashed more power in the complex, but let's wait and see if he shows it against better arms before we get too excited.

The Risks: High. Roederer has only a complex league resume and may end up in a corner outfield spot.

Bret Sayre's Fantasy Take: Herding prospects in a dynasty draft without the requisite fantasy upside we're looking is like herding "Cattle" in that there's safety in numbers when it comes to deeper formats. There are always a handful of guys like Roederer every year who don't look like they have a notable fantasy future but take an unforeseen step forward in pro ball. You just can't roster all of them.

9. Brennen Davis OF

OFP: 50 Likely: 40 ETA: 2024
Born: 11/02/99 Age: 19 Bats: R Throws: R Height: 6'4" Weight: 175
Origin: Round 2, 2018 Draft (#62 overall)

The Report: Davis has louder tools than Roederer, but significantly more rawness in his game as well. He looks every bit the basketball player he was for much of high school, and his frame is extremely projectable—which is to say, he's skinny. The frame and swing portend significant raw power, but everything is very mechanical at present, and he doesn't really have the strength to drive the ball without yoking up for it yet. He's a plus runner with a strong arm, so if he can stick in center, you could be cooking with gas here in a half decade or so, but the lead time here is likely to be significant. I do have a weird thing about ex-basketball-players though (Amir Garrett and Monte Harrison jump to mind…welp), so I can't help but like Davis, even if we could share jeans at this point.

The Risks: This is closer to extreme than high, so let's just go very high. He's raw even by prep outfielder standards and has only briefly focused full-time on baseball. There's a fair bit of positive variance here too given his inexperience and projectability.

Bret Sayre's Fantasy Take: If Davis were a "Photograph," he'd take so long to develop that the photo store you brought the film into would have closed down, turned into a dry cleaner, then the dry cleaner would have gone out of business and been replaced by a store that fixes electronics but has such a terrible and kitschy name that you couldn't imagine going in there without feeling shame.

10. Alec Mills RHP

OFP: 45 Likely: 40 ETA: Debuted in 2016
Born: 11/30/91 Age: 27 Bats: R Throws: R Height: 6'4" Weight: 190
Origin: Round 22, 2012 Draft (#673 overall)

The Report: I have a soft spot for Mills, even though he stretches the definition of "prospect" as far as anyone on any list. A bone bruise on his pitching arm cost him most of the 2017 season, or else he would have likely already established himself as a useful Swiss Army knife for the Cubs pitching staff. If you need him to start, he has four pitches at the offer. Granted, the curve is a slow strike-stealer with a bit of 12-6 depth, and the slider is inconsistent and can back up at times, but it's improved enough to be a useful, perhaps even average major-league offering.

Mills can also come in out of the pen and give you a couple innings, leaning more on his low-90s fastball and change. The two-seam version of the heater shows sink and run and he spots it down in the zone well. The change works well off the heater with 10 mph of velocity separation and late sink. The total package here is on the fringy side—and given the profile, you'd like to see a longer track record of throwing strikes—but he had his moments both as a starter and reliever late last season in Chicago. Mills is a useful piece for your pitching staff that I've always liked more than most (and perhaps more than I should).

The Risks: Low. Doesn't get much more finished product than a 27-year-old who debuted in 2016.

Bret Sayre's Fantasy Take: "Barely (If At All)". Sometimes when these things work, they really work. The Brewers' list is going to be better. I promise.

Others of note:

Brendon Little, LHP, Low-A South Bend

Little struggled last year during his first minor-league season. The command was inconsistent and his fastball velocity was down from what was reported last year. The fastball actually looked quite pedestrian, sitting in the low-90s with little movement. A serviceable third pitch also never developed, and instead Little relied solely on his fastball and curve.

There is some optimism for a rebound in 2019. Little's strength is the curveball, which features 12-6 shape and sharp break. He's confident enough to throw it in any count and will bury it to get batters to chase. The Cubs hope some minor mechanical changes will solve the troubles that plagued him at South Bend. Lacking an effective third pitch, the profile looks like it's destined for a bullpen role.

Jhonny Pereda, C, High-A Myrtle Beach

Overshadowed by Amaya, Pereda quietly had a solid season as Myrtle Beach's backstop. He doesn't have Amaya's loud offensive tools but he's worked diligently with Chicago's minor league staff to become a legitimate catching prospect. He's athletic and agile behind the plate with one of the best arms in the organization. Offensively, he has a solid approach and some sneaky pull-side power. He looks like a glove-first backup, but with continued development at the plate, Pereda could become the Cubs' next breakout catching prospect.

Jose Albertos, RHP, Low-A South Bend

Man, I thought for sure I would have been writing about Albertos much further up this list and even on the 101. Pitchers are notoriously risky, but if you were gonna bet on it going bad for Albertos it would have been injury-related, not suddenly walking 20 per nine. His calling card had been polish and advanced fastball command in 2017, but that was nowhere to be found in 2018. And this wasn't just generic wildness: this was "often not in the same zip code as the strike zone" wildness. There have been arm concerns with Albertos before, but this doesn't appear to be that. The yips aren't insurmountable, but there's a better chance I skip this section entirely next year than spend time trying to fit Albertos onto the back end of 2020's Top 101.

Chicago Cubs 2019

Top Talents 25 and Under (born 4/1/93 or later):

1. Ian Happ
2. Albert Almora
3. Addison Russell
4. Miguel Amaya
5. David Bote
6. Victor Caratini
7. Alex Lange
8. Adbert Alzolay
9. Aramis Ademan
10. Justin Steele
11. ~~Addison Russell~~

These past few years, writers on this list have had things pretty easy. Reserve the top six or seven spots for core big-leaguers, sprinkle in some intriguing low-level guys, and call it a day. It's become a little more complicated this year, with the last World Series starters aging off and a farm system that has been depleted by trades. There are still a few guys at the top who will get major-league at-bats this year, but the talent drops off fast.

Since losing Dexter Fowler, the Cubs have struggled to replace his bat at the top of the order. The opportunity was ripe for either Ian Happ or Albert Almora to fill the void and cement their place as part of Chicago's core. But neither completely gained Joe Maddon's trust.

Happ's rookie campaign was solid, with a 111 DRC+ and the defensive versatility that the Cubs love. His sophomore season was less so, as his strikeouts skyrocketed and the power faded. The hope in Chicago is that 2018 was an aberration and that the bat will return to form.

Almora appeared to be having a breakout 2018 season, slashing .319/.357/.438 and playing exceptional centerfield defense. However, an extended July slump and a rejuvenated Zobrist cut into his playing time down the stretch. Again, there's plenty of hope: his bat is solid and he plays a mean centerfield.

David Bote spent seven years in Chicago's minor-league system as an unheralded prospect before reworking his swing and finding his way onto the 40-man roster. He filled in nicely for the injured Kris Bryant and even provided one of the best highlights of the year with his walk off grand slam against Washington. Like many rookies, he hit a wall when scouts figured out his weaknesses, and he'll need to make adjustments to thrive. It's unlikely that he will ever have a positional home given the stars in Chicago's infield, but he's versatile enough to fill in almost anywhere on the field and provide some pop at the plate.

On a team with a deeper farm system, backup catcher Victor Caratini probably doesn't make this list. There's not a lot of upside remaining in his game but he does provide value as a switch-hitting catcher who can fill in at a corner infield spot when needed.

Part 3: Featured Articles

The Hole in The Shift is Fixing Itself

Russell Carleton

I've been on a bit of a mission against The Shift of late. I'm not out to get The Shift for the usual reasons that people oppose it. The words "the right way to play the game" won't be found on my lips. If a team wants to pursue a strategy that is within the rules and it works, then by all means, they have my blessing (not that they need it). Instead, my concern with The Shift is a worry that it doesn't work, or at least that it has a flaw that needs fixing.

The data show that while The Shift does a decent job of preventing singles on balls in play (what it's supposed to do), it also increases the number of walks that happen in front of it, and the number of additional walks outweighs the number of singles saved. It's a problem because you can't throw a guy out if he gets to walk to first base.

But the "why" was important. It seemed that The Shift was changing the way in which pitchers pitched. We saw that there were fewer fastballs thrown in front of The Shift than we might otherwise expect, and that pitchers tended to stay out of the strike zone a little more. Not by a lot. In fact, it might not even be visible to the naked eye. The percentage of pitches that are out of the zone goes from 51.0 to 53.3 from a standard defense (two right/two left) to a full shift (three on one side). That difference stands up even after we control for the types of hitters that get shifted against. And it's enough to drive up the walk rate to where it cancels out the benefits that teams thought they were getting with The Shift... and then some.

But there was some hope. I found that when individual pitchers stayed closer to the in-zone/out-of-zone mix that they used without The Shift on, they could still get the benefits of The Shift without the walk problems. So, in theory, a team could simply figure out a way to convince its pitchers to not fall prey to the walk trap and The Shift would once again be their friend.

It's reasonable to think that some teams might be more hip to this idea than others. Maybe some figured it out a year before the others. Maybe they were better at getting the message across to their pitchers. Or, maybe no one has figured it out yet.

Warning! Gory Mathematical Details Ahead!

I used data from 2015-2017, made available through MLB's data portal, Baseball Savant. They are kind enough to note when teams are using an infield shift (three fielders on one side of second base), as opposed to a "strategic shift" (someone's playing a bit out of position, but it's not quite that drastic) or a "standard" alignment.

Since we're doing this by team, I can't just look at raw walk rates, because we know that some teams have good pitchers and others have not-so-good pitchers. Some have a mix of both. I used the log-odds ratio method to take into account a batter's general walking proclivities, and a pitcher's as well, and then shoving them into a binary logistic regression. Then, I asked the computer to generate a specific coefficient for each team's pitchers, for when they went into The Shift and how that affected their walk rate.

Using those coefficients, I was able to project what would happen if a league-average pitcher faced a league-average hitter (which we expect would product a league-average walk rate; from 2015-2017, 7.7 percent of plate appearances ended in a walk) and then just switched his hat. Here's the top five and the bottom five:

Top 5 Teams	Projected Shift Walk Rate	Bottom 5 Teams	Projected Shift Walk Rate
Rockies	6.2%	Rangers	11.2%
Pirates	6.7%	Mets	10.4%
Indians	7.2%	Dodgers	10.2%
Astros	7.3%	Cardinals	9.9%
Braves	7.7%	Tigers	9.7%

There are probably people out there right now trying to figure out what the common thread is among the top and bottom teams. I'm sure, because this is Baseball Prospectus, people are already trying to make the case that sabermetric "early adopters" have some sort of edge here. I think that the more interesting piece is that by the time you get to fifth place in The Shift, we're at league average.

As a sanity check, I examined the issue on a pitch-by-pitch level, looking at how often pitchers threw their pitches in the GameDay strike zone, and again using the same basic methodology and getting team-specific coefficients. The names on the list re-arranged themselves, but the idea was the same, and the two lists correlated with an R of .593.

There's a reason that I don't usually do this type of leaderboard post. I don't really know what the Rockies, Pirates, Indians, Astros, and Braves have in common, or what they have that the bottom five don't. I can put a shrug emoji here and say, "Well, it must be something!" but that seems like a cop-out. Instead, I'd like to present another table and suggest that the table above doesn't even really matter anymore.

Year	League Percent Outside K Zone (Full Shift)	League Percent in K Zone (No Shift)	Difference
2015	54.1%	51.1%	3.0%
2016	53.3%	50.9%	2.4%
2017	52.6%	50.9%	1.7%
2018	52.0%	50.7%	1.3%

The hole in The Shift is fixing itself, and it's coming down really fast league wide. In my earlier work on The Shift, I suggested that until teams stopped having such a huge difference between their out-of-zone rate with and without The Shift on, there would just be too many walks for The Shift to make sense. It seems that all 30 of them have been working toward just that. I once estimated that it takes about 10 years for an idea to filter its way through baseball. At this rate, it looks like teams are going to catch up a lot faster than that. And yeah, they're all saber-smart now.

It's likely that whatever magic it was that the Rockies and Pirates had has made its way to Texas and Queens. Or is at least on its way. And if teams are committing to fixing the walk problem, then it's likely that they will continue shifting and shifting a lot.

And eventually it's going to actually make sense for them to do it.

—*Russell Carleton is a former author of Baseball Prospectus and now an analyst for the New York Mets.*

The State of the Quality Start

Rob Mains

One of the seven things you (probably) didn't know about the 2018 season is that quality starts—defined as a start lasting six or more innings with three or fewer earned runs allowed—as a percentage of total starts cratered to an all-time low of 41 percent. I want to look a little more deeply into this, since it's been a while (May of 2016, to be exact) since I've examined quality starts.

The term *quality start* is credited to *Philadelphia Inquirer* sportswriter John Lowe. It's been derided ever since he coined it in December of 1985. Three runs in six innings? That's a 4.50 ERA! In what world is that a measure of quality?

Let's start with that criticism. It's true that 3 x 9 / 6 = 4.5. (You came here for this sort of high-level math, right?) But it's also true that type of start, meeting the bare minimum for earning a quality start, is unusual. Here's the proportion of quality starts in which the pitcher lasted exactly six innings and yielded exactly three earned runs. (I'm going to confine this analysis to the 30-team era, 1998-present. Almost all data retrieved in this article is via the Baseball-Reference Play Index.)

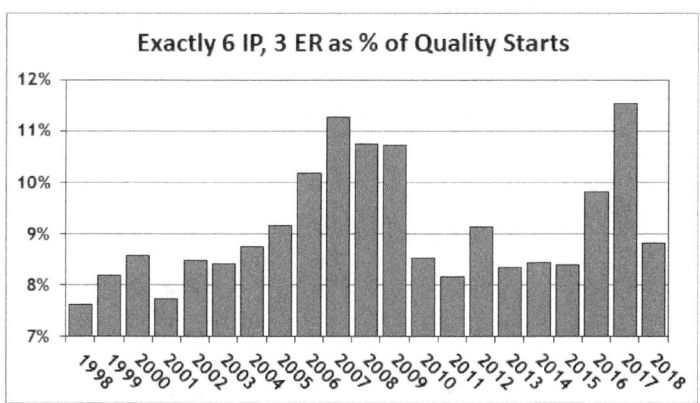

There were 1,997 quality starts in 2018. Only 176, or fewer than one in 11, featured a pitcher going six innings and allowing three earned runs. Put another way, the percentage of quality starts that resulted in a 4.50 ERA (8.8 percent) is less than half the percentage of games in which a batter hit two home runs and his team lost (22.5 percent; 237-69 won-lost). That doesn't impugn hitting two homers.

So if a 4.50 ERA isn't the norm, what is? How good are quality starts?

Pretty good, it turns out. First, on a team level:

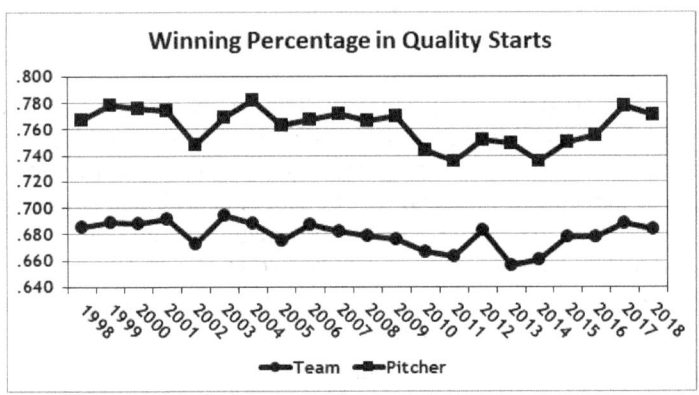

Teams receiving a quality start from their pitcher won 68.4 percent of their games in 2018, in line with the 30-team era average of 67.9 percent. A team with a .684 winning percentage wins 111 games. Getting a quality start is definitely a good thing. Individual pitchers throwing quality starts have a higher winning percentage because a big slice of team losses is assigned to a reliever.

If teams do well in quality starts, how well do the starting pitchers do? Again, very well.

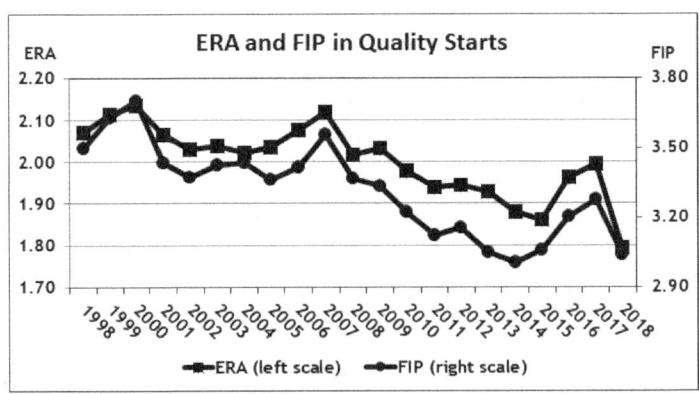

Pitchers in quality starts had a 1.79 ERA (blue line) in 2018, *the lowest in the 30-team era*. Their FIP was higher, 3.04, but still excellent. In the 30-team era, only 2014 had a lower FIP for quality starts, 3.01.

But, of course, the run environment in 2014 was different. Teams in 2014 scored 4.07 runs per game, the fewest in a non-strike year since 1976. They scored 4.45 runs per game in 2018. So surrendering a 3.04 FIP in 2018 is more impressive than 3.01 in 2014. Accordingly, let's look at ERA and FIP in quality starts relative to league averages.

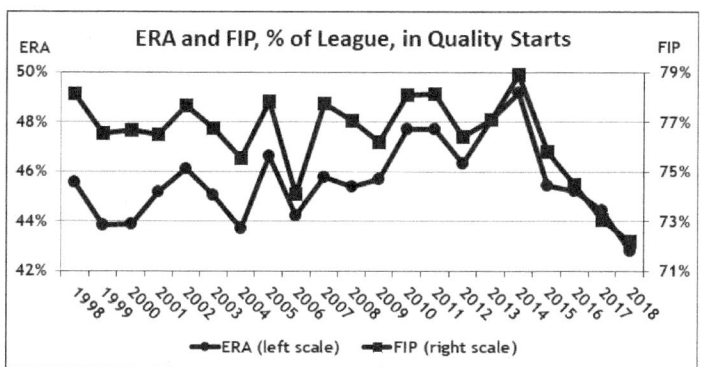

This tells a more dramatic story. Starting pitchers in 2018 gave up a 4.19 ERA and a 4.21 FIP. Starters in quality starts gave up a 1.79 ERA, 43 percent of the league average. Starters in quality starts gave up a 3.04 FIP, 72 percent of the league average. Both of these marks represent lows in the 30-team era.

The takeaway here is this: *Quality starts are better, relative to other starts, than they've ever been over the past 21 years.*

Maybe during the winter I'll look at this over a longer arc of time. For now, though, we can definitively say quality starts are the best they've ever been since the Diamondbacks and Rays joined the majors.

Yet, paradoxically, they're down.

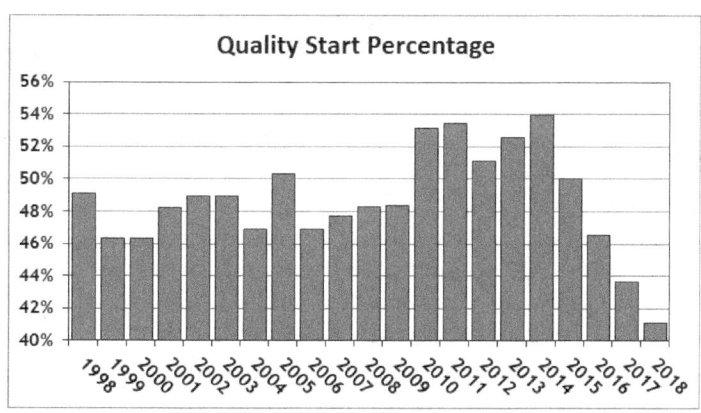

This graph covers only the 30-team era. In my article last week, though, I looked at the years 1908-2018. The result was the same. The 41 percent of starts in 2018 that were quality starts are an all-time low, well below the runners-up: 1930's 43 percent (the year teams scored an all-time record 5.55 runs per game) and last year's 44 percent.

The normal explanation for a dip in quality start percentage is an increase in scoring. When teams score a lot of runs, it's harder for starting pitchers to last six or more innings and limit opponents to three earned runs. From 1998 to 2014, the correlation between runs scored per game and the percentage of starts that were quality starts was -0.94. That means there was an extremely close relationship: More runs, fewer quality starts. Too small a sample? Go back to the start of the Expansion Era, 1961, and the relationship is even more negative, a -0.95 correlation, though 2014.

But that's broken down over the past four years:

- 2015: Runs per game increased from 4.07 to 4.25, quality start percentage decreased from 54.0 to 50.1. Yes, that's a negative relationship, but the regression model would predict a decline of 1.5 percentage points. We got 3.9 instead.
- 2016: Runs per game increased from 4.25 to 4.48, quality start percentage decreased from 50.1 to 46.6. Past experience would suggest a decline of just 1.8 percentage points. We got 3.4.
- 2017: Runs per game increased from 4.48 to 4.65, quality start percentage decreased from 46.6 to 43.6. Again, the direction's right, but the magnitude isn't. Using the relationship from 1998 to 2014, that increase in scoring should've reduced quality starts by 1.3 percentage points, not 2.9.
- 2018: Runs per game declined from 4.65 to 4.45. That should've resulted in the quality start percentage moving in the other direction, rising 1.6 points. It didn't. It fell 2.6 points, as noted, to an all-time low.

Granted, we're talking about just four years here. Maybe they're outliers. But I don't think they are. Quality starts, as noted, are as good or better than ever. But they're rarer than ever as well. And I think I know why.

To get a quality start, you need to allow three or fewer earned and pitch at least six innings. That's 18 outs. Here's a graph showing the number of starting pitchers who limited their opponents to three or fewer earned runs but got pulled after pitching at least five innings but fewer than six:

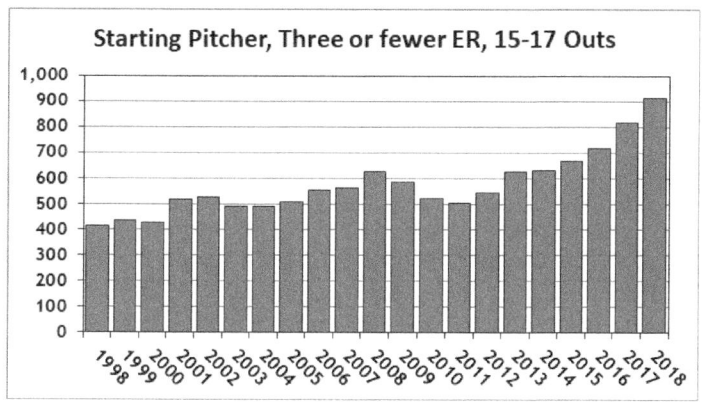

A pitcher getting 15 outs pitched five innings. A pitcher getting 16 outs pitched 5 1/3. A pitcher getting 17 outs pitched 5 2/3. More than ever before, pitchers are being removed from games in which they are within 1-3 outs of a quality start, falling just short of the six-inning finish line. Widespread acknowledgement of the times-through-the-order penalty and a flotilla of available bullpen arms is making the quality start simultaneously both more excellent and more rare.

Which is ironic, given that we saw a new post-war quality start record this season:

Rank	Pitcher	Season	Consecutive QS
1	Jacob deGrom	2018	24
2	Bob Gibson	1968	22
-	Chris Carpenter	2005	22
4	Johan Santana	2004	21
5	Luis Tiant	1968	20
-	Mike Scott	1986	20
-	Jake Arrieta	2015	20
8	Robin Roberts	1952	19
-	Tom Seaver	1973	19
-	Jack Morris	1983	19
-	Greg Maddux	1998	19
-	Josh Johnson	2010	19
-	Jon Lester	2014	19

While there have been longer streaks spread over multiple seasons, no pitcher since World War II threw more consecutive quality starts in one year than Jacob deGrom this year. The fact that he did in a year in which quality starts were the rarest they've ever been adds to the accomplishment.

—Rob Mains is an author of Baseball Prospectus.

Heads-Up Hacking—The First Pitch

Matthew Trueblood

Batters fell behind in a higher percentage of all plate appearances in 2018 than in any previous season for which we have pitch-by-pitch data. That kind of granular information goes back only to 1988, but we might safely assume (given all we know about baseball as it had been before that, and as it has been in the years since) that batters have *never* fallen behind at a higher rate than they did last season.

Through the 1990s, the percentage of all plate appearances that began 0-1 hovered in the high 30s and low 40s. In the 2000s, it rose steadily but slowly, through the mid-40s. In 2018, 49.8 percent of all trips to the plate began 0-1. That, as much as anything, captures in microcosm the nature of hitting in MLB today.

A countdown clock toward strike three begins ticking almost the moment a batter takes his place in the box. The league's adjusted OPS+ on the first pitch was higher in 2018 than ever before, and that has been true in most of the last 10 seasons. Batters hit .264/.289/.442 in all plate appearances in which they swung at the first pitch last season, and .241/.330/.395 in all plate appearances in which they took that first offering.

The percentage differences in batting average and isolated power there favor swinging at the first pitch by more than in any season since 1988, while the difference in on-base percentage favors taking by more than ever. If you want to get on base at a decent clip, it's a good idea to be patient, but you run the risk of missing the only chances you'll get to produce power.

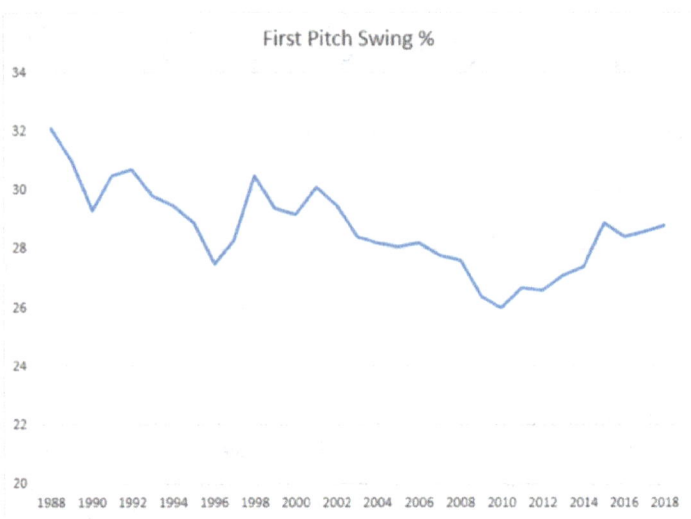

The league swung at the first pitch 28.8 percent of the time in 2018. With the isolated exception of 2015, that's the highest that number has climbed since 2002, but it might not be high enough. With the help of BP research maven Rob McQuown, I looked at the aggregate Called Strike Probability (CSProb) on the first pitch for each season since 2008, when the implementation of PITCHf/x first made measuring that possible. It's risen sharply during that period.

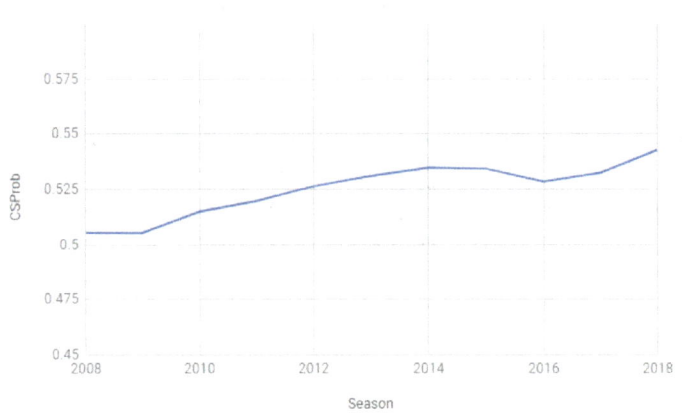

Called Strike Probability, First Pitch of PA (2008-2018)

Called Strike Probability is exactly what it sounds like: a pitch with a given CSProb has roughly that chance of being called a strike, if not swung at. In 2018, a batter who took 100 first pitches from a random sampling of the league's pitchers might expect to fall behind 54 or 55 times—up from 50 or 51 times in 2008. Almost regardless of pitch type (and, notably, especially in the case of fastballs), the first pitch tends to have more of the zone right now than ever before.

Pitchers are better at throwing strikes. They have better stuff, and believe more in their ability to miss bats within the zone. Perhaps most importantly, they know that batters are looking for one thing on the first pitch: a fastball. If they don't get it, they're likely to take the pitch. Check out how the use of sinkers and four-seamers on the first pitch has changed in a decade:

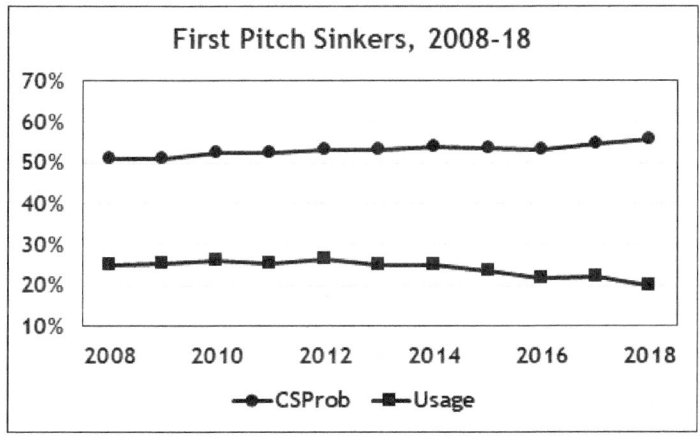

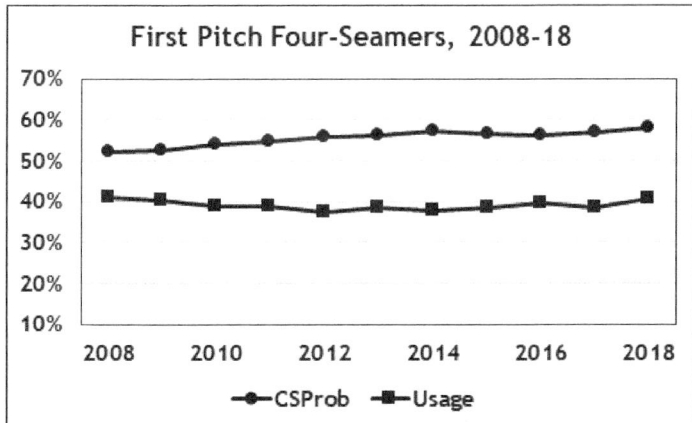

Chicago Cubs 2019

The sinker is losing its place in baseball, but the rate at which pitchers have thrown it on the first pitch hasn't dropped any faster than its usage rate in other counts. Pitchers have actually gone to their four-seamer *more* often to open counts, in the last few years, after a dip in the 2012-2015 period. What's really changed, though, and what shows up in both charts above, is that pitchers are catching more of the zone with first-pitch fastballs than they were a decade ago, or a half-decade ago. They're attacking right away, even with the pitch they know batters are expecting. The message is pretty clear: batters are being too passive.

Sliders, curves, and changeups each have more of the zone when thrown on the first pitch than they did several years ago, too, though the effect is less pronounced. Pitchers have seen the numbers; they know batters are doing better on the first pitch itself. They still feel safe throwing more and better strikes than ever before, figuring they'll come out ahead as long as they keep getting ahead to open each battle.

The Moneyball revolution brought an increased league-wide focus on OBP, which resulted in a de facto mandate to take a more patient tack at the plate. It worked very well for a while, as batters with poor plate discipline were compelled to either adjust or be expelled from the league, and pitchers with poor control were slowly weeded out.

However, concurrent with that revolution, and spurred by it in some ways, was the evolution of the pitching paradigm that now dominates the game. As batters ratcheted up their focus on inflating pitch counts and working walks, pitchers honed theirs on throwing strikes and missing bats. The league's understanding of what makes a good pitcher improved at least as much, from the mid-1990s through the mid-2000s, as its understanding of what makes a good hitter. As amphetamines and other performance-enhancing drugs were phased mostly out of the game, and as PITCHf/x broke onto the scene, individuals and teams learned how to exploit the evolved approaches of even the smartest hitters.

The ability to avoid making outs is still the most valuable one in baseball, but the magnitude of its eclipse of slugging is smaller than ever. To a greater extent than power, on-base skills derive their value from chaining—from the on-base skill levels of the players on either side of a given individual. Eleven years ago, when the housing crisis hit, people learned the hard way that the value of their homes depended a good deal on the values of their neighbors' homes. The same wasn't true, though, of their cars. So it is now, with OBP and SLG.

The global OBP in 2018 was .318. The only seasons since the Dead Ball Era in which the league got on base at a worse clip were 2013-2015, 1988, 1971-1972, and 1963-1968. This is all happening despite the aforementioned evolution of the science of hitting. It's happening despite a shift in approach and focus, one that would steer OBP ever higher, if only it were working.

Instead, it's sitting at a low ebb, and while it does so, even guys who get on base often are a little less helpful than they were 10 years ago—or 20, or 40, or 60, or 70, or 80, or 90. They're less helpful, that is, because unless there happen to be three or four other guys in the lineup who get on just as regularly, their contribution is merely to forestall the inevitable. Runs happen, increasingly, when a sudden bang happens, and that means attacking early in the count—because pitchers are sure as hell doing that.

In a league making contact on barely 75 percent of its swings, and a league in which an increasing number of pitchers can throw multiple off-speed pitches for strikes in any count, the only way to consistently generate offense is going to be aggressive. This isn't necessarily true for individuals, like Mookie Betts and Jose Ramirez, who make a lot of contact and have excellent plate discipline, and whose power comes from such natural quickness in a short stroke. Most players have to make tradeoffs, though, whether it be lowering their contact rate or raising their chase rate, in order to consistently make the quality of contact necessary to survive in today's game.

Highest %	Lowest %
Javier Baez – 48.3	Joe Mauer – 4.6
Freddie Freeman – 47.1	Mookie Betts – 9.7
Ozzie Albies – 46.3	Brett Gardner – 10.7
Jose Altuve – 44.2	Jose Ramirez – 12.0
Nick Castellanos – 44.1	Jason Kipnis – 13.8
Joey Gallo – 42.3	Jesus Aguilar – 14.5
Corey Dickerson – 40.9	Xander Bogaerts – 15.8
Salvador Perez – 40.8	Brian Dozier – 16.3
Eddie Rosario – 40.7	Mike Trout – 17.6
Nick Ahmed – 40.4	Yasmani Grandal – 17.6

Top 10 and Bottom 10 Hitters, First-Pitch Swing Rate (2018)

The question isn't which of these lists one prefers, but what they each convey, qualitatively, about the cat-and-mouse game of early-count hitting. Those top five on the left, especially, drive home the fact that for most players, getting aggressive early in the count is now key to keeping strikeout rate down and hitting for power.

For now, the message is: pitchers are coming right after batters with the nastiest stuff they've ever had. Batters had better stop giving away strike one and force hurlers to adjust, or the global OBP crisis is only going to get worse.

—*Matthew Trueblood is an author of Baseball Prospectus.*

A Hymn for the Index Stat

Patrick Dubuque

We survived without computers. I know this, because I remember the day when my dad hooked up his brand-new Atari 400 computer to the back of our 12-inch Magnavox television, and the perfect blue of the memo pad lit up for the first time. I was born just on the edge of that transitional generation, of learning cursive and balancing checkbooks and just doing math all the time, constant manual arithmetic.

It still amazes me. We learned how to sail ships without computers. We learned how to do calculus. We built towers that didn't fall down, most of the time. We engineered catapults to knock them down anyway. We built a robust system of philosophy called "utilitarianism," founded on the principle that the good of an action is evaluated by summing the effects of that action, which is the kind of formula that would make the world's mainframes crash. The whole foundation of statistics as a field is "here's math you could easily do but would die of old age first."

The fact of the matter is that there is too much math in the world to do. There are too many things changing, and too many things too small to notice, for us to handle. At some point, they become too much for the computers to handle as well, which is why we have chaos theory and undetectable earthquakes, but it's not an even fight. At some point, we fall back on intuition, and given how under-equipped we are, we're forced to bestow that intuition with some sort of supernatural superiority, the "gut feeling," that we can't prove because we can only intuit that our intuition is better.

We're all lousy at intuition, and wonderful at lying to ourselves about it. The honest truth is that computers are far better at intuition than we are, because in order to know what feels "off" you have to know what's "on." In order to do that you have to constantly reassess the average of everything, then re-rank your own experience against it.

Test your own, by comparing these three anonymous lines:

Player	G	HR	AVG	OBP	SLG
Player A	156	38	.259	.342	.535
Player B	154	38	.280	.348	.527
Player C	158	38	.266	.343	.509

These all seem like pretty similar players, right? The second one a touch more batted-ball dependent, the third a little less strong, but all pretty good hitters. And you'd be right, about the latter. Not the former.

Here's the breakdown:

- Player A: 1991 Howard Johnson, 141 DRC+
- Player B: 1996 Dean Palmer, 121 DRC+
- Player C: 2018 Giancarlo Stanton, 114 DRC+

Baseball is fortunate to have escaped the seismic shifts of so many other sports, where the talents and performances of other eras are nearly unrecognizable. (And not just other sports: try to explain the greatness of the movie Duck Soup without adjusting for era.) But they're still there, and they're nearly impossible to account for manually, without having to resort to sweeping generalizations like "steroid era" or juiced-ball era" to throw out entire swathes of production.

This is all to say that we should celebrate the index stat, that simple 100-based scale with such a humble aim: just to give context. It's hard to imagine how we lived without them for so long. Sabermetricians have always tried to make their stats look like other stats: True Average mapped to batting average, FIP molded to look like and compare to ERA. It's easy to understand the motivation—these statistics carry an emotional value in them that is hard to resist, as with the .300 hitter and the 2.00 ERA—but even they fall prey to the same loss of scale as their unadjusted counterparts. If a .300 average means different things in different years, does that hold true for a .300 True Average?

Instead, 100 doesn't say anything, except above average or below. And it does it instantly, for every season in every run environment for any statistic we want it to. We should have more index stats: K%+, so we can stop comparing Mike Clevinger's career 9.46 K/9 to Nolan Ryan's 9.55. HBP%+, so we can note that Ron Hunt was getting plunked when nobody else was getting plunked, as opposed to that imitator Brandon Guyer. Some might note how stale these references are and accuse league-adjustment as a backward-looking drive, and this is true. But we're always looking backward, always comparing the new with the expectations already set. The index stat just forces us to be honest.

There's always resistance to a new statistic, especially one so outwardly simple and so internally complex. We tend to stick with what we know, even in the case of formulas that are supposed to tell us what we know. But if your resistance is that it seems too complicated, too counterintuitive, too "black boxy," I encourage you to consider why you feel that way. Because the real world is infinitely more complicated than baseball, where all the pitches go in one basic direction and the baserunners are only allowed to travel in four directions. Baseball statistics based on mixed methodology are almost impossibly intricate. So are skyscrapers and automobiles. That's why we have computers—to take the guesswork out of them.

—*Patrick Dubuque is an author of Baseball Prospectus.*

Index of Names

Abbott, Cory 99
Adduci, Jim 96
Ademan, Aramis 89, 106
Albertos, Jose 99, 109
Almora, Albert 22
Alzolay, Adbert 93, 105
Amaya, Miguel 90, 104
Arcia, Francisco 96
Baez, Javier 24
Barnette, Tony 49
Bote, David 26
Brach, Brad 51
Bryant, Kris 28
Caratini, Victor 30
Cedeno, Xavier 99
Chatwood, Tyler 53
Cishek, Steve 55
Clarkin, Ian 99
Clifton, Trevor 99
Contreras, Willson 32
Darvish, Yu 57
Davis, Brennen 96, 108
Davis, Taylor 96
De La Cruz, Oscar 99
Descalso, Daniel 34
Dewees, Donald 96
Duensing, Brian 59
Edwards Jr., Carl 61
Evans, Phillip 96
Field, Johnny 96
Graveman, Kendall 63

Hamels, Cole 65
Happ, Ian 36
Hendricks, Kyle 67
Heyward, Jason 38
Hoerner, Nico 91, 103
Hultzen, Danny 99
Kintzler, Brandon 69
Lange, Alex 99, 104
Lester, Jon 71
Little, Brendon 99, 109
Maples, Dillon 73
Marquez, Brailyn 99, 107
Mills, Alec 75, 108
Montgomery, Mike 77
Morrow, Brandon 79
Norwood, James 81
Pereda, Jhonny 109
Quintana, Jose 83
Rea, Colin 99
Rizzo, Anthony 40
Roederer, Cole 96, 107
Rosario, Randy 85
Rucker, Michael 99
Russell, Addison 42
Schwarber, Kyle 44
Short, Zack 96
Steele, Justin 99, 106
Strop, Pedro 87
Tazawa, Junichi 99
Thompson, Keegan 99
Tseng, Jen-Ho 94

Uelmen, Erich	99	Wilson, D.J.	96
Underwood, Duane	95	Zagunis, Mark	92
Vasto, Jerry	99	Zastryzny, Rob	100
Webster, Allen	99	Zobrist, Ben	47
Wick, Rowan	99		

Ballpark diagrams for Baseball Prospectus are created by THIRTY81Project, a design concept offering original ballpark artwork, including the new 'Ballparks of 2019' 11 x 17 color print.

Visit **www.thirty81project.com** for full details.

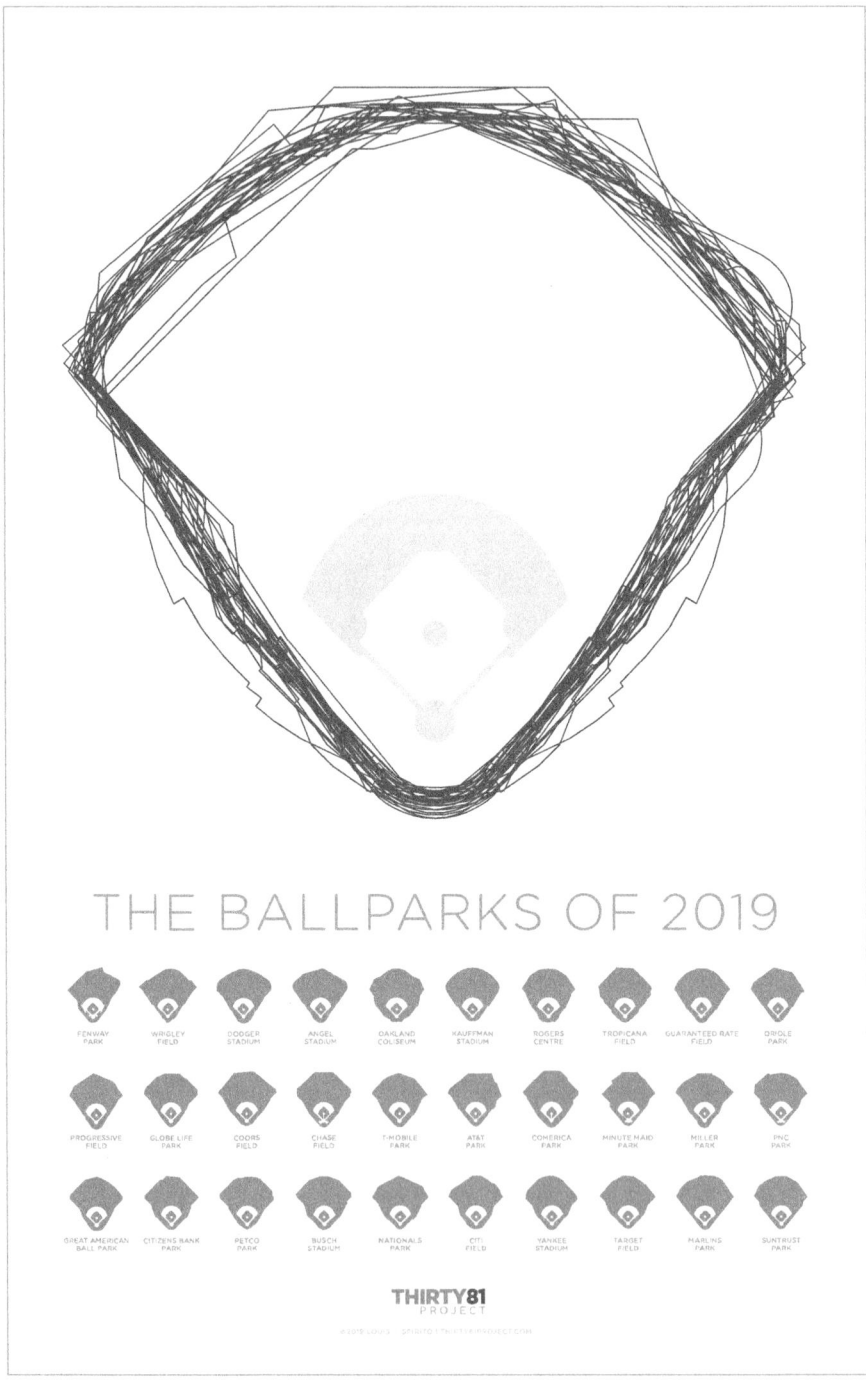